THE MOBILE MANAGER:

A Study of the New Generation
of Top Executives

the mobile manager

a study of the new generation of top executives

EUGENE EMERSON JENNINGS

Professor of Management

Graduate School of Business Administration
Michigan State University

McGraw-Hill Book Company

New York • St. Louis • San Francisco • Düsseldorf • Johannesburg
Kuala Lumpur • London • Mexico • Montreal • New Delhi
Panama • Rio de Janeiro • Singapore • Sydney • Toronto

The Mobile Manager

Library of Congress Catalog Card Number: 67-65498

07-032450-6

First McGraw-Hill Paperback Edition, 1971

PRINTED IN THE UNITED STATES OF AMERICA

To my son, Peter

Foreword

This book is the first attempt of the author to present the fledgling technique of mobilography. Hopefully, it will some day become acknowledged as a science. As such, it will attempt to describe the positions through which managers of large industrial corporations pass as they go to the top, and to make predictions based upon these descriptive data. The main intent of this first effort is to introduce new categories that describe the characteristics and problems of mobile managers today. There is no attempt however to indicate how many managers may belong to each of these new categories. These categories are presented with the hope that they will enable the reader to see different dimensions to the problem of becoming an effective manager. If there is one finding that has come from mobilography, it is that managerial effectiveness is based upon mobility. This generalization represents the kind of statement made frequently in this book and is presented as a hypothesis upon which much mobilographic research is presently based and will be based in the future. This report is based upon 1,500 managers and executives selected from 500 large industrial firms and 230 presidents who held office during the sixteen years over which this study was made.

The author wishes to express his indebtedness to his assistant, Mr. Donald Smart, who helped prepare the frames for publication and provided valuable technical assistance in the mobilographic studies.

The author wishes to thank the Bureau of Industrial Relations, University of Michigan, for the opportunity to test the language of mobilography with hundreds of managers attending their institutes, seminars, and conferences. The opportunity has enabled the author to see the communication problems involved in translating research argot into practical language.

The author wishes to express his appreciation to his wife, Marilynne, for her invaluable effort in preparing the manuscript and guiding it through to completion.

Eugene Emerson Jennings
East Lansing, Michigan

CONTENTS

CONTENTS

Chapter I

THE MOBILE HIERARCH

During the period before the middle of this century, a boy dreamed the American dream of success and woke up hoping that it would come true. The men who were successful were heroes to him, assaulting aggressively the corporate slopes, and winning out against great odds. For generations, a very few went to the top, some went part of the way, while others never became managers at even the first level above the worker. Then the unheralded economic growth of the last two decades set in motion the unprecedented forces of rapid upward mobility. The result was the largest group of young executives that our economy has ever seen, and following them closely are even more youthful and mobile managers. For them, and the many who are to follow them, the American dream is no longer a dream; it is a reality.

As this new force of unprecedented mobility quietly took hold, it carried to the top of this great economic wave many men who themselves expended amazingly little effort, and who were sometimes promoted in spite of their deficiencies. So vast were the demands for talent that men often times became eligible for promotion or transfer simply because they were available. This expedient approach signaled the state where corporations grew faster than they could develop the talent necessary to serve the requirements of sustaining that growth.

The implied assumption of management development generally shared by businessmen before this period of economic growth was that talent would automatically declare itself through application of skill and industry to work much as cream rises to the top of milk. This natural law worked adequately during periods of mild economic growth, but corporations came to realize that during a long period of sustained growth the corporation could not wait for nature to produce adequate numbers of talented managers. By the middle of the fifties, a few corporations started to interfere with the natural law of talent development and to rush it along by careful nudging, and at times downright violation, of the law itself. More corporations gradually bowed to necessity. By the early sixties the growth corporations had become extremely pleased with the superior product of a managed program of management development. The so-called natural law of talent development became a relic of a past generation, to be replaced by new theories.

The theme that has absorbed the conscientious efforts of the new generation of managers is found in the principle: mobility equals competency. It is now a widely established fact that most jobs can be mastered in a year and a half to two years and that from then on the manager is doing the work with a minimum of effort. If he is moved to another job, masters its requirements, and is moved to a third job, he can, in a few years, get more intensive training and development than the previous manager, who usually stayed in any one job long after he had mastered its fundamentals. In pre-mobility days, the manager was taught his job the way a child was taught the piano: practice made perfect. The manager went over and over his work, each time grinding out a little more perfection at a tremendous cost of career time.

Today the men at the top are products of compressed experience, the stresses of which not everyone was able to stand. In fact, the mobile manager has left behind a large number of casualties. We seldom hear from them because many have given up the struggle and now sit quietly and dutifully on carefully prepared shelves. They represent the passed-over generation. Like his mobile counterpart, the passed-over manager spent his childhood in the depression, his youth and early manhood in the period around World War II, his creative energy in the fifties, and his money in the sixties.

While similar in many ways to his mobile counterpart, *the passed-over* manager is different in several respects. He is grateful for his limited mobility but terribly confused. In this period of unprecedented, rapid, upward mobility, when he should have gone higher, he did not; yet he does not know exactly why he did not. When the American dream was more hope than expectation, the passed-over manager could explain limited mobility by appeal to chance or bad luck. Today, he runs the risk of rationalization if he ignores the overpowering evidence of the vast number of men who have gone farther and higher than he has at a much younger age.

One question that is relevant to the men of the passed-over generation is, "Will they live to make sixty?" The mobile manager has exploded the myth that the ulcer level exists at the corporate zenith. The fact is that the incidence of psychosomatic illness is significantly higher among members of the passed-over generation, as well as the premature death rate due to heart attack and suicide. The stresses that the passed-over men incur can be aggravated partly by the successes of the mobile manager. For many, stress without success has become unbearable during this period of high mobility.

The vast majority of men at the top today have been carried up by an economic tidal wave, although the fact that some of them would have surfaced anyway is, indeed, a logical assumption. But the vast majority were produced. If they had one particular quality, it was that they were ready and responsive to mobility. They had the fast responses, the capacity to drop one thing and pick up another, to leave one position and arrive at another with the knowledge that they must be ready to depart again shortly.

The passed-over generation had as much energy, ability to concentrate, belief in the efficacy of hard work and cold hard realism. What they lacked was a mental set that geared them to the wave of mobility, that gave them the inspiration to live mobility as if it were a central value.

The men at the top now constitute the first generation of mobile managers. They believe strongly and uniformly in the efficacy of mobility. Whereas the pre-mobile manager believed that hard work made men better, the new manager believes that mobility makes men work better. The mobile manager enjoys the compression of experience, is challenged by the routine of mobility, and seeks to remain mobile. The economic scene exerted a selective influence that screened out the men who could not endure the stresses and strains of compression experience. And now these managers, the products of high mobility are ensuring the survival of the new generation of managers by assiduously applying the principle that mobility breeds competency of a quality greater than that of hard work.

The new generation of mobile managers is the child of economic affluence and rapid upward mobility. The step-child is the science of mobilography. Corporations cannot purposefully and systematically develop managers and executives without at some time asking the question, "Through what kinds of positions do these men pass on the way to the top?" Corporations are beginning an era that will find a prodigious amount of effort aimed at discovering the answer to this question. Success in discovering the routes to the top will produce the ability to predict movement to the top. The invention of the science of mobilography has been as much a creature of necessity as has been mobility itself.

The day is not too distant when the electronic computer, which can direct a space vehicle, solve a complex scientific problem and match an aggressive boy with a passive girl, will be used to identify and place highly mobile, effective managers and executives. Computers will scan the resumés of managers and executives at a rate of hundreds a minute and issue instructions to prevent and remedy the problems that have been largely beyond the grasp of personnel departments of large business corporations. The talented manager lost in the corporate maze, the mobile executive going too fast up the corporate ladder, the promising manager who is without proper training and development, the executive headed for a career crisis—these and many other perplexing problems will be attacked successfully by the science of mobilography.

This newly discovered tool is the study of the mobility patterns of managers and executives, the routes they take to the various levels of the corporation, including the topmost echelons, the distribution and number of mobile managers, of slow and fast movers and of their delays and difficulties en route. The argot of mobilography will allow the corporation to condense the careers of all of its managerial and executive personnel into a capsulized format that will allow easy inspection of differences in mobility patterns and rates. Members of a large corporation will be able to see at a glance the hundreds and thousands of men who move in all the far flung corners of the corporation. Imagine for a moment, the president of such a corporation being able to watch the race to the top as conveniently as he can watch on a warm summer afternoon a horse race at his favorite track.

It is odd that with all the emphasis today on developing managerial personnel, little effort is given to discovering who is progressing and regressing and at what rates. The large corporation invests millions of dollars each year on the training and education of managerial personnel, but does little to determine who are the real beneficiaries. The science of mobilography will bring a rare degree of precision and refinement to the process of managerial development.

The science of mobilography is based upon the need to know who are the most upwardly mobile men in the corpo-

ration and to compare them with the least upwardly mobile. A mobility audit will be essentially extensive and
intensive in scope. By extensive, we mean that all men at
all levels will be surveyed to discover the kinds of jobs that
they occupied during their careers in the corporation. By
intensive, we mean that the occupants of select positions in
the corporation will be studied for as far back as twenty to
thirty-five years, and their mobility patterns determined.

Mobilography is basically concerned with the men who
move into the offices of the executive suite and with their
career backgrounds. Men who have filled the offices of president and vice-president for several administrative generations will be audited intensively. The mobility audit of
corporate officials for the past several decades will provide
a base for evaluating relative rates of upward mobility. It
will provide a set of routes that transport men from the
bottom to the top. With these bases of comparison, managers at the many lower levels in the corporate hierarchy may
be evaluated and classified into super-mobiles, sub-mobiles,
and arrested mobility types, depending upon their rates of
upward mobility.

Any science is dependent upon having useful categories.
Fifteen years of studying mobility patterns of executives in
the 500 largest industrial corporations have provided a few
useful distinctions. First there is a group of business executives at the top who are entrepreneurs. They are the men
who built the corporations from the ground up and who
still preside over them although with the passage of time,
there are naturally few remaining entrepreneurs in large
industrial corporations. There are many more sons of entrepreneurs (SOE) who are at the top because of their birth.
We have also discovered a large number of grandsons of
entrepreneurs (SOSOE) who reside at the top and a few
sons-in-law of entrepreneurs (SILOE).

Sons, grandsons, sons-in-law and other men related by
birth or marriage to the entrepreneurs are categorized as
birth elite. They have entirely different rates and routes of

mobility than does a group of business executives called hierarchs.* These are the men who have moved from the bottom to the top without any family or marriage connections operating for or against them. A pure hierarch is to be differentiated from a lateral hierarch who moves into the top from another corporation. Lateral hierarchs as well as birth elite have interesting and informative mobility rates and routes, but they should be analyzed and evaluated separately from pure hierarchs. A pure hierarch is one who has emerged or is emerging from within the same corporation where he started his career. A recent report on the chances of becoming a corporation president failed to make these distinctions between birth elite, lateral hierarchs, and pure hierarchs, and consequently proved to be both misleading and lacking in the precision necessary to predict movement to the corporate zenith. Mobility studies of men who have moved into the executive suites of the 500 largest industrial corporations during the last twenty years show that a majority of executives (pure hierarchs) move through the corporate hierarchy in a predictable pattern of three definite stages:

> 1) the technical level which is non-managerial and subsumes the work of salesman engineer, scientist, accountant, etc., 2) the managerial level which advances from supervising non-managers through managing managers to finally taking the responsibility of a corporate division, and 3) the executive level which is made up of the president, his immediate subordinates, and the men who report directly to these immediate subordinates. These may be either line or staff men.

The majority profile in mobility studies shows an S curve.

The pattern of a specific executive may be a bit jagged,

---

*The author is indebted to several of his colleagues for the term hierarch. They include Orvis Collins and David G. Moore.

but the patterns of executives collectively average out to form this S curve. We call the technical phase an entrance stage to a managerial career. The future president started as a specialist in sales, personnel, engineering, or accounting. The average president who is a pure hierarch spent no more than three years in the technical, non-managerial stage. One-fourth of them were spotted and elevated within a year and a half, and one-fourth were spotted within three to four years and elevated into the entrance stage. The average relative time (ART) is one and one-half years for the most mobile (super-mobile); two to three years for normals; and three to four and one-half years for the slowest (sub-mobiles).

The second stage in the mobility cycle of the pure hierarch is called developmental. Here the future president moves up rapidly through middle management, tending to move around laterally as well as upwards. This stage is acute mobility, to say the least, and provides the corporation with well-rounded executive talent. The future president moves through the positions in middle management fast, and he moves sideways frequently. Because he moves around as he moves up, the mobile executive has a sort of upward spiral pattern to his career. Generally, the future president who is a pure hierarch does not stay in one position more than eighteen to twenty-one months. The super-mobile stays on the average of fourteen to eighteen months and the sub-mobile, twenty-one to twenty-eight months.

The last stage of the mobile hierarch's route to the top is called arrival. This stage is measured by how frequently and with what duration the individual interacts with the president on a face-to-face basis. As we have noted, he is generally on the arrival pad when he assists (line or staff) a man who sits on the president's first team (executive committee). One-fourth of the presidents (pure hierarchs) were appointed to the office between the ages of 47-49. Most held the reins between the ages of 50-53 and one-fourth at the age of 54 or older. Hence, the super-mobile's average age when president (AAWP) is 49, or less, that of the normal mobile is 50-53, and that of the sub-mobile is 54 and over.

From these averages we can derive an overall average relative time (ART) for each of these three stages.

	Super-Mobile	Normal Mobile	Sub-Mobile
Stage 1*	0-2 years	2-3 years	3-4 years
Stage 2*	11 years	14 years	15 years
Stage 3*	8 years	10 years	17 years
Total	21 years	24 years	32 years
AAWP**	47	50	54
Cutoff	49 or younger	50-54	54 or older

* In mobilography argot these three stages are entrance, developmental, and arrival.
**Average Age When Made President

A super-mobile is one who becomes division president and general manager before the age of 40, a normal mobile achieves this between 41 and 48, and a sub-mobile at 48 and older.

It must be noted that the ART is a basis of comparing the rate of movement of men in a corporation. This factor must ultimately be based upon data obtained from within the corporation itself. National figures are helpful to compare with corporate rates and routes. Average relative times will be obtained at all levels in the corporation of super-mobiles, mobiles and sub-mobiles.

After monitoring a large number of pure hierarchs who have become presidents of the 500 largest industrial corporations during the last two decades, some general patterns have been detected. These findings are subject to more thorough study by mobility auditing of specific corporations. As yet, no one total corporation has been mobility audited although divisions and departments of several corporations have been. The following general findings, many of which will be examined in greater detail, will serve to orient the reader to subsequent material.

Mobilographical Findings

1. Mobility and corporate strategy are highly related. The routes and rates of mobility change with the strategy of the corporation. The change from a manufacturing emphasis to a marketing orientation has enlarged the number of managers moving to the top in marketing and sales and from these kinds of backgrounds. Marketing and sales produces more presidents than accounting, finance, personnel, corporate law, and manufacturing. Together manufacturing and marketing produce 41 percent of pure hierarchs at the top. As the research and development budgets have increased, so have the number of people at the top increased with scientific and engineering backgrounds. They now number about 18 percent but are gaining rapidly in number.

The route to the top has changed as the corporation has developed a multi-national orientation. In the period from 1948-1953, few presidents had three or more years in foreign operations. By 1966, one out of three presidents had been three years or more in foreign subsidiaries and divisions. As the corporation has increased the emphasis upon planning, evaluating, problem analysis, research, and advisory activities, staff positions have become developmental. In 1948-1953, only 25 percent of the presidents (pure hierarchs) had more than five years in staff assignments. Today, only 25 percent of the presidents have had less than five years during their managerial careers in staff work of some kind. It is no longer believed that only line managers provide presidential stock.

2. Men at the top strengthen their own mobility routes. The top executives tend to bring with them crucial subordinates who have largely the same mobility patterns, and thus routes become strengthened by and through the successes of men who have created them. Points one and two actually work against each other at times. Men at the top may be replaced by men from other routes because of changes in corporate strategies. Changes in corporate

strategies, however, do not occur suddenly, partly because of the threat to existing routes of mobility. The dependent variable seems to be corporate strategies. For this reason, corporations often adopt new strategies long after the facts warrant changes. It has often been noted in mobilography that success is more than merely turning in consistently high performances. There are also more slowly moving routes to the top in which there are many good men. There are many good managers in accounting and personnel, but these routes produce the fewest number of pure hierarchs at the top.

3. There is a strong relationship between mobility and competency. We have already made reference to the fact that the requirements of many, if not most, managerial positions can be learned in a year and a half or less. Mobile executives have an 80/20 orientation toward most positions. By this is meant that 20 percent of any job counts for 80 percent of the learning. If they can master the 20 percent and move on to another job, the learning curve is constantly rising. If they were to stay in the job longer, they would be completing the 80 percent of the job that counts for only 20 percent of the learning. Besides, much of this 80 percent can be mastered easily from the transfer knowledge that has accumulated during previous managerial experiences. Only about 20 percent of a new job is actually new and developmental. The manager who can move into a position, grasp its essential uniqueness and master the new responsibilities and assignments, and move to another job is apt to gain more competency. Many managers after a year and a half are doing their jobs without the utilization of their full talents and energies, and each additional year decreases their mobility rate, increases lost career time, and slows down their developmental curve. Because men were kept in jobs long after they had learned them, they overlearned their jobs on each rung of the corporate ladder. They were not only slow in arriving at the top, but when they did many were old men with much

of their enthusiasm and brilliance wrung out of them. Today, things are becoming radically different. Promising managers are moved before they get bored, and if anything, they practice underlearning. They have to be mentally alert to get into a job, to learn quickly its fundamentals and to move to another job.

4. Mobility is highly related to growth. The firms that have had spectacular growth patterns have had high rates of mobility of all kinds. They have had high functional mobility. Men move up fast through the functions of business, accounting, finance, personnel, manufacturing, marketing, sales, research, and development. In response to a growth need, a trend started in the early fifties to move managers across functions: for example, from engineering to sales, from accounting to manufacturing, and so forth. Now these growth corporations realize that men who stay in one functional route all the way up suffer from limited route vision. They see the whole corporation from the various viewpoints of their functional routes with sometimes deadly results. This can be lethal. The most mobile pure hierarch who has crossed several functional routes is a product of them and has a much wider scope.

Growth corporations have increased the rate of mobility in their divisions. They have also started to move managers from one division to another to prevent restricted vision. The cross functional mobility and cross division mobility patterns are becoming so common among growth firms that few men will arrive at the top by 1970 who are not products of both types of mobility.

Growth firms have as well increased geographical mobility. Managers are moved to different areas of the corporation to expose them to similar responsibilities in different social, economic, and political environments of the corporation and of society. They often substitute geographical mobility for positional mobility.

In the arrival stage, assignment mobility is often substituted for positional mobility. In growth firms, the executive may stay in a position longer than he did at managerial levels, but he will have three to four times the number of special assignments or task-force responsibilities.

5. Mobility is largely a relationship between two or more people. An outstanding quality of the men in the arrival stage who eventually become presidents is that they have the capacity to trust and to be trusted. Few men arrive at the top who are not trusted by somebody already there. They move up by being sponsored by someone who has the power to promote or recommend promotion.

This means that successful executives move into the arrival stage largely with the help of others. Executives move up in twos and threes bringing with them their key subordinates, who are considered crucial to their superior's effectiveness and mobility. They know how to make their superiors look good and how to keep them moving ahead, and in this way they move ahead too.

The mobile executive must know human character or he will invest energy in the wrong people. The key subordinates are highly competent, dependable people, not "yes" men. They fill in their superior's deficiencies and overcome their superior's weaknesses. As one president who retired recently points out, "An individual is not selected for the presidency because of his personal skills alone, but because he has a team of two or three crucial subordinates or colleagues who together provide a package of skills needed by the corporation for its next five year program."

This means that a new kind of president is emerging, the project type. These are men who are asked to do a particular job, after which they turn the baton over to the next executive in the relay race. This means that they stay in the job about five years or less. Ten years was the average tenure of presidents (pure hierarchs) in our base period (1948-1953). The trend is such that by 1970, 50 percent or more will be project presidents.

Executives become presidents because corporate situations require their talents. A corporation has a kind of rhythm of its own that determines the movement of talent. To execute project assignments successfully, the manager must know how to organize teams of limited purposes and to draw talent from the far corners of the company. As a project manager, he must motivate people who have their loyalties attached to their superiors and functions. After the project is completed, the team will disband and its members will return to their former assignments or get new ones. The nature of business today requires an endless array of projects that call upon specialized talent from all over the corporation. So common are projects today that few men arrive at the top without having served on them many times. Through projects and subordinates, crucial subordinates are made.

6. Mobility is related to entrance age. During the last fifteen years the large industrial corporation has increased the amount of scarce resources (money) it has devoted to managerial personnel. Whereas there are four times as many people interacting on a face-to-face basis with presidents during a week period in line and staff positions, the presidents have not had their salaries increased as much as those of their immediate and twice removed subordinates.

Mobilography has a term called early arrival (EA). Operationally, an early arrival is a manager who makes his age in salary. If he is thirty-five years old, he is making a base salary of thirty-five thousand dollars or more. A few mobilographic studies of this pattern reveal the distinct possibility that the large industrial corporation is placing its scarce chips on a particular kind of individual. He is one who early in his career displays a capacity to manage. There are four times as many early arrivals today than there were in 1948-1953. Managers are being paid more to manage managers. Relatively speaking, the salaries of the very mobile manager have increased far more than the salaries of executives and presidents. It is now estimated that 15 percent of all managers below the executive or arrival stage are making their age in salary. Furthermore, 14 percent of all managers in their thirties are making thirty thousand dollars or more in contrast to about 4 percent in 1948-1953. The most mobile managers are relatively young for their salary level and positional level. The chances of making thirty thousand dollars a year are four times as great for the man who gets out of the technical or entrance stage in two years than for a man who stays there five years or more. To put it another way, a man who performs non-managerial tasks five years or more has a decidedly greater improbability of becoming a high wage earner.

Contrary to what some people believe, the men who fail at the top are not the men who came up fast. Mobilography has a research term called early terminal (ET). This refers to a president who stayed in the job less than half the average relative time of about five years. Any president who has stayed two years or less has usually been summarily relieved of his job. Of some ninety-six early terminals, only one-fourth could be classified as having been early arrivals and super-mobiles. The most were delayed arrivals, having spent too much time in middle management jobs. Having overlearned their jobs, they spent too much time in middle management jobs. As presidents they showed in their managerial styles an inability to adapt quickly and to respond to change and crisis. There is something deadly about staying in middle management too long. The biggest step in the corporate ladder is from executive to president. This last step cannot be approximated by any prior training, except perhaps by throwing managerial assignments to a promising manager just as fast as he can absorb them.

The men moving to the top today are compression products. They have ranged far and moved up fast and have had compressed into them an intensive and varied set of experiences in a very short period of time. It takes, today, 70 percent of the pure hierarchs twenty years to go from first level manager to president, during which time they will be moved geographically seven times and positionally eleven and will receive countless numbers of special and project assignments. There is no room for the man who cannot catch on quickly and gain the necessary self-confidence required to sustain performance at higher levels.

Of course, mobility may exceed skill and self-confidence. One of the bad effects of the last fifteen years of economic growth and high managerial mobility is that many managers have moved up faster than they have acquired skill and self-confidence. They have, as a result, drawn stays and demotions and recline on shelves for the rest of their careers. The number of executives and managers who were once very mobile but who now sit on shelves is fantastically large. Mobilographic estimates at this time suggest that the number of shelf sitters in the large industrial corporation is three to five times as great as it was in the early fifties.

During the last fifteen years of this huge, unheralded, growth cycle, corporations have produced the youngest generation of top executives our economy has ever had, as well as the largest number of arrested mobility types below them. Of course, not all can be mobile. The corporation needs men who can manage well at all levels. After all, not everyone can go to the top or maintain upward mobility. However, many shelf sitters became marginal effectives (ME). A marginal effective is a manager who is perceived by his evaluators as doing just enough to get by. Life on a corporate shelf whittles away at his drive and ambition. After sufficient time, the manager becomes marginal. The corporation is littered with marginal effectives. We seemingly know very little about how to motivate a person to work effectively and well in the same job for many years without reawakening his desire to go higher. The tolerances are very close between the amount of motivation required to work hard and the amount that will cause the subordinate to acquire false hopes for the future. Many supervisors cannot successfully motivate marginal effectives within this narrow gap.

In short, the men who have moved to the top spent little time waiting to be identified as potential managers. They were spotted as managerial potential when they were technicians. At each level above the first level supervisor they arrived earlier than expected and sustained their drive. Few sat on shelves or committed errors from which they could not successfully rebound. They arrived early at the top with reputations for being able to take as much as their supervisors could throw at them. The old cliché, "Give the work to the busy guy if you want it done," is certainly applicable to them.

7. Mobility is related to building a reputation. The men who move to the top have reputations. They are known for doing things differently. Contrary to the prevailing stereotype that success is based on conformity, the mobile manager is an innovator. He stands out from the mass as a person with unique ideas. But he is more than an idea man. He knows how to innovate and at the same time keep the support of his superiors, not always an easy task. If there is a conformist, it is the manager who will not attempt to persuade his superior to try a new idea. Many scientists and engineers believe that the better half of creativity is coming up with bright ideas. The mobile manager knows that the better half of creativity is selling a bright idea to a superior. Many corporations are loaded with men with bright ideas who cannot effectively sell them to others. The mobile manager has acquired not only a reputation for selling, but also for executing the idea and making his boss look good.

Mobility is largely a transaction in which one thing is exchanged for something else. The subordinate makes his superior look good and in turn expects his superior to make him look good before those higher up the scale. Of course, these acts are committed under the agency of silent understanding. Many subordinates do not know how to cue their superiors to keep up the other end of the bargain. They are simply incapable of transacting this exchange of expectations. They do not seem to understand that they must initiate the transaction and that this is done by giving their superior something to talk about to his superior in turn. The superior is not going to report something ordinary. To qualify, the report must be about innovative results. Hence, the process of making the superior look good is essentially carried out by giving him something to talk about to his superior.

Mobile managers claim that at times superiors have been so unwilling to change that the managers have had to assume in advance full responsibility for failure before their superiors would give final approval to a new project. Many an unwilling superior has been carried on the back of an eager subordinate as he runs the risk of innovation.

Far too many managers are reluctant to argue their innovative interests over a protracted period of time. They try once or twice and give up in a huff, placing the blame upon their superior for being rigid. Mobile managers are terribly persistent. They are not infantile or vulgar, but they have a tenacity that borders on fixation. They become successful because they cultivate rather than bulldoze. This means that they do their homework, carefully arrange and present the facts, impersonalize their arguments, and never back their superiors to the wall. They thrust and parry with their attention on any sign of beginning acceptance.

Almost all men who move to the top keep their superiors alert with innovative efforts, many of which are rejected, but all of which cause their superior to pause and seriously consider and reconsider. Looking back, they will tell the mobility auditor that many of their best ideas were the most difficult to sell. Now they understand why every idea that comes down the pike cannot be accepted. There just are too many good ideas that innundate an executive. Many of them are gems in the rough, and because the subordinate is aware that they must be sold, he is forced to polish them up and fight for them vigorously.

Reputations are based partly upon seeing the very minor possibilities in front of one's nose. Few mobile managers have ground out major innovations at the exclusion of minor ones. If anything, they have an overpreponderance of minor innovations of the kind that when discovered appear to be insignificant. They are the things that almost anybody could see if he were bent on seeing the very apparent. Some managers hope to discover the very big ideas and fail to try their skill with the small. The mobile manager shows a rare ability to concentrate and a patience with minor innovations. He is aware that a major program could come as a spin-off of a seemingly trivial notion. The mobile manager has a style of success, pressing hard on the corporate boundaries, but never losing the rare knack of keeping the support of his superiors.

8. Mobility is not directly related to intelligence. The men moving the fastest do not have a corner on the brain market. They are not significantly more intelligent (as measured by standard intelligence tests) than immobiles. Intelligence seems to be uniformly scattered throughout the hierarchy. The reason for this even distribution is that most of the men who are capable of managing have higher than average intelligence quotients. The distribution of their IQ scores is truncated. This means that in a situation where the individuals have above average IQ's other things become more important. For that matter, decades of scientific research by behavioral scientists have failed to isolate one trait or quality that reliably predicts success and failure. Not even the most reliable test, namely intelligence, has been validated. Reliability has been substituted for validity. That is to say, the psychologist does not know what the intelligence test is measuring, but whatever it is, the test is measuring it consistently. Perhaps the future will provide tests that have validity and we will be able to

report then that some kind of intelligence does separate the men from the boys.

If we did know that men at the top were significantly more intelligent, it would not make the problem of managing managers any easier. The very bright people vary more among themselves in many personality characteristics than do people of average intelligence. Among the brightest subordinates, the manager is just as apt to find an aggressive extrovert as a depressed introvert. The problem of managing bright managers could become a stupendous problem that itself could outstrip the gifts of the very gifted. In any case, mobility and intelligence are far from reciprocals of each other at the present time.

Because intelligence tends to relate to college grades, it is to be expected that the latter do not predict mobility, which is indeed the case. But first, let us point out that the number of college degrees among managers is increasing rapidly, as it is in our society in general. In 1948-1953, 80 percent of all the men at the top of large industrial corporations and 65 percent of the pure hierarchs studied had bachelors' degrees. By 1965, 95 percent of the former and 85 percent of the latter were college graduates.

But often a bachelor's degree is no longer enough. In the 1948-1953 period, eight percent of the men at the top had master's degrees; by 1963, 33 percent had master's degrees; in 1964, 37 percent; and in 1965, almost 40 percent. At the present time, 21 percent have earned doctorates. The projection shows that by 1970, 60 percent of the presidents will have master's degrees and 30 percent doctorates. Pure hierarchs are close on the heels of these statistics. Of course, some industries lag in their share of college graduates and advanced degree holders. On the whole, we may expect that presidents will look for equivalent or more education in their successors.

In the period of 1948-1953, training programs were not common. Today, they transport more and more from college into management after a two or three year development program. In addition, mobile managers on the average acquire 600 hours or more in development programs between the time they leave college and before they become presidents. These seminars keep them technically and managerially alert. Each year at least 35 presidents out of 100 attend seminars devoted to managerial training of some kind.

If then there is one single factor that separates the new breed of executive from his predecessor, it is that he considers managing a learning experience. He is open to ideas, knowledge, and education; he seeks to use the latest technological devices to improve the art and science of managing people. He is willing to expose himself to any skill, job, superior, or project that will hasten his opportunity to get more challenging assignments.

Today, 75 percent of the most mobile men have bachelor's degrees in engineering or science and master's degrees in business administration. Men with this combination of degrees are out-distancing any other combination. With his bachelor's and master's degrees, the aspiring executive is best prepared to enter the first phase of his career in the corporation, the entrance stage.

The question is, what does the higher incidence of undergraduate and graduate degrees mean? It means that the corporation is exerting a selective influence that favors men with college degrees, although it does not follow that college grades cause mobility. If anything, college grades can be a handicap. The routes to the top are apt to hold just as many or more men who graduated below the highest one-third of their college class than above (on a per capita basis). Also, it appears that the number of scientists and engineers who were demoted in two years from first level management back to non-managerial levels is almost twice as great for those with A— or better college averages than for those with a B minus average and less. There is growing evidence that if a scientist or engineer has a master's degree in business administration, his chances of staying in the position of first level manager are much better. It should also be suggested that if the A minus or better scientist or engineer gets past the second level, the probability of mobility is equal to that of any graduate in another field. Although mobilographic studies are much too inadequate to present these findings as anything more than a hypothesis, a large number of corporations report that they have suspected for some time that the managerial roles were exerting a negative effect upon the bright college graduate in science or engineering. It is commonplace to find that men who have been well trained in college in some professional area such as engineering or science hope to pursue their careers in as pure form as possible. Many professionally trained people have aspired to their vocations as early as ninth grade. Many years of hard work under rigorous educational situations reinforced in their minds the professional halo that gradually took over command of their adult personalities. This hold upon them of the images and values of their professions is keenly seen when the young engineer, scientist, or accountant discovers upon entry into the business world that so much of what he has been taught is not practiced or useful in business. The author has watched the agony undergone by young men who discover that business and industry do not really use engineers in the way in which they have been trained. The struggle to maintain one's professional identity is a story that has not been adequately told. The well educated engineer or scientist conceives managing as alien to his interests. He usually looks down his nose on managers and, in most cases, he does not respect them because they do not measure up to the high standards of technical competency that he holds. The reader can imagine the look that he gives a manager who asks him if he would consider a supervisory assignment.

Men who enter first level management have a mental technical-managerial mix. For example, they may believe that 90 percent of effectiveness is based upon technical competency and 10 percent on organization, motivation, communication, and other skills of management. A mix overly concentrated on technical competency is exceedingly common among young managers with strong technical backgrounds. They rely only upon their technical expertise and discount any managerial skill that may be applicable. Perhaps one of the reasons a student who does less than excellent work in college goes up the managerial ladder faster is that he went to college primarily to gain entrance into a managerial career. He majored in a technical area because he knew that it would open the door to a route to the top, but dissipated his energies with many non-technical interests. The highest grades are earned as much by unswerving hard work as by brightness, and the student who sets himself more than the single goal of A grades can not normally afford the concentration necessary for that kind of achievement.

9. Mobility is related to leveraging. The mobile manager tends to be impatient with success. He wants as much as he can possibly get in the shortest period of time possible. When he sees that his upward mobility is blocked by a slow moving superior, he may try to advance the rate of his mobility by leaving the corporation and joining another. Or he may leverage because he has made some grave mistakes and he feels he cannot overcome them by any amount of excellent performance.

The leverage rate among managers at all levels has increased substantially in the last two decades and particularly in the last ten years, even at the top levels. It is roughly estimated that two out of five presidents are lateral hierarchs. These men have moved into high levels of the corporation from other corporations. Leveraging may not be appreciated by the corporation, and in fact, some corporations will not hire back managers who have quit. In the few instances that they do, the managers are usually penalized by inferior positions and salaries.

However, leveraging may serve a productive function to

the individual and society. It allows individuals to keep up their mobility pace and it helps in the process of distributing skills to various sectors of our economy and society. There is much talent wasted because managers and corporations will not find better channels for the employment of managerial skill. Many managers stay in corporations long after they have had their upward mobility arrested permanently. There are companies that could use their skills more efficiently if these men were capable of leveraging. To be mobile, one must not become permanently identified with any one corporation. The trend is that by 1970 every president will have leveraged at least once, and 60 percent will have leveraged twice.

So common is leveraging that the mobile manager considers himself to be a professional who hires himself out to a corporation for an indefinite period of time. The old saw of hard work and devotion to corporation is disappearing rapidly with the advent of mobility. Professionalism has replaced employeeism. So highly common is leveraging, that an unprecedented number of executives and managers are being placed by executive placement firms sometimes called "headhunters." Such placement firms are not to be disparaged as they are basic to a mobile society.

The problem of leveraging is that too many managers fail to inspect carefully the corporation which they have recently joined. They find that they have been deceived or misled and usually leverage again. The second leverage uses up valuable career time. When carefully executed, leveraging can be a vital key to mobility. Without it, the mobile manager necessarily reduces his options and his chances of upward mobility.

10. Mobility is creating mobicentric managers. Mobilographic interviews and studies reveal a manager whose central concern is for mobility itself. During the last fifteen years of high economic growth and upward mobility, mobility has become for many a value. (Men who keep on the move have little time to get into trouble). Success is mobil-

ity. It is not so much position, title, salary, or exceptional performance as it is success in moving and movement. In mobicentric circles, it is not power or money or position, but getting positions and leaving positions that counts. And when one cannot go up, one can enjoy a ride to the side. This is one reason why the leverage rate has increased drastically in the past ten years. The pleasure of movement to the side in order to enjoy the pleasure of leveraging up is a most fulfilling exercise today. The mobicentric does not ask to stop the world to get off. Rather, he asks to stop the world so that he can get back on. Any minor amount of non-movement is displeasure to him. He wishes every part of himself to be in simultaneous motion; he thrusts himself totally into activity. But it is more than activity; it is direction—movement.

To the mobicentric individual, the most important activities in life are preparatory to mobility. School, college, marriage, social life, and even religion and faith are central to mobility. Most young people join the church today to achieve activity. The term they use is to become meaningfully involved in a responsible organization, but the central idea is to become and stay active. In a mobicentric society, non-movement is anathema. The price for non-movement is loss of identity. We can see this loss of identity in managers who have had their upward mobility arrested.

The anxiety and anguish of drawing a shelf or a demotion is apparent to the auditor. Imagine what it must be like for a manager who has shot through five levels of management to have to go back down to absorb a failure in the midst of managers whom he has left behind. His first reaction is to leave the corporation, and he often does to avoid humiliation.

Although the exit rate is very high on a shooting star type, it would be higher if it were not that corporations lock-in a manager during later stages of his upward mobility pattern by pensions, bonus, and seniority benefits. He must settle for financial security, but the pain of no movement cannot be entirely assuaged by these measures. The result is that many men who should exit do not and suffer intensely in their forced inactivity. Some keep the hope alive that they can once again enjoy the thrill of movement which may be partially achieved through geographical change. Some may actually become mobile again, of course, and these few will tell you the difficulties they experienced as shelf sitters while solving problems that never needed to be solved.

The profile of a mobicentric is a manager whose style of managing is predicated upon rapid movement from position to position. He never expects to complete a job, is prepared to depart soon after he arrives, is impatient in doing the finishing stages of an assignment, is preoccupied with the mobility of people about him, is quick to feel mild anxiety when he stays in a job too long, rejects the belief that a person can move too fast, definitely does not believe that he has moved or is moving too fast, refers himself psychologically to people several levels above him who are fast climbers, tends to be somewhat aloof with superiors who are slow climbers, demands a great deal from subordinates, and sees a direct relationship between their efforts and his mobility rate, and tends to seek and accept assignments that give him high visibility.

Mobilographic studies show that managers cannot relax and feel a sense of achievement after they receive a promotion. Actually, they wait to see what follows their promotion. A stay too long in the same job (Stay) or a lateral transfer could undo their promotion. Between the two, a lateral transfer after a promotion counts more than a lateral transfer after staying a long period in the same position; and a stay that follows a promotion is worth more toward mobility than one that follows a lateral transfer. If this logic is given to mobile managers, they will uniformly agree to its veracity. The author seldom meets a hierarch who disagrees with the logic that a lateral transfer is worth more to him than a stay, regardless of the intrinsic importance of the work to him.

In conclusion, the mobile manager is a novel fact of corporate existence. He undergirds the entire economic structure and is producing men like himself. We shall next examine in more careful detail the elements of mobility with special reference to middle managers.

Chapter II

THE SPONSOR SUPERIOR

Mobility is a partnership between the manager and his corporate environment, but this matching does not exist solely between himself and his work requirements or between himself and his superior. Mobility is a product of a wide arrangement of contacts, opportunities, and relationships that extend to the whole corporate activity. The corporation now breeds the manager, but in the era preceding the mobile manager, subordinates developed because of the relationship they held to their immediate superiors. Managers were believed to be born, not made, and their application to work was a sign of their native talent.

Superiors and subordinates were basically work oriented and managers were promoted when positions were vacated. The relationship between work and promotion followed the traditional logic that the one necessarily preceded the other. Hard work was the necessary basis of promotion, and the latter was more a reward after the fact than an incentive to achieve the fact. Few superiors realized the possibility that promotions could be the necessary cause of high performance. Even if they did realize this possibility, they were kept from applying it by the inability to extract a promotion for a deserving subordinate and, more important, to receive a promotion themselves for developing a promotable subordinate. The ethic was not yet established that the superior should never leave a position to a subordinate less effective than himself. Superiors were not then placed under the gun to produce future superiors.

The work ethic of the time kept subordinates as subordinates and superiors as superiors. Work was delegated in such a fashion that routine assignments went to subordinates and major assignments were reserved for superiors with the result that the gap between the two was carefully maintained. Superiors always deserved promotions, subordinates were always awarded them. The amount of development that a manager received was largely based upon the willingness of his superior to vary his work assignments. Whatever new assignments were given were relatively routine in nature and were held to a minimum consistent with work efficiency.

In the preceding chapter we have examined the basic reasons why the work ethic has been replaced by what we may call the developmental ethic. The manager today has the responsibility of developing talent as good if not better than his own.

For this reason, one way to be assured a promotion is to have excellent replacements ready and waiting. Their need to maintain their developmental rate will exert pressure upon the corporation either to promote the superior or to transfer the talented subordinates. The latter possibility requires that other superiors be responsive to the developmental needs of managers. In this way the whole corporation graduates her managers to various degrees of proficiency.

We shall next examine some of the elements that produce mobile managers. The reader should keep in mind that these factors are basically resources that mobile managers and growth corporations utilize as part of the growing ethic of managerial development.

Visibility and Exposure (Visiposure)

One of these elements upon which mobility is dependent is visibility. Its usual meaning of having the ability to be apparent at sight is used in a special mobilographic sense to describe the relationship of subordinates and superiors. Upward visibility is the opportunity to see superiors while to be upwardly visible is to be in a position of being seen by superiors. We shall call latter position *exposure* to differentiate it from upward *visibility*. It does not necessarily follow that high exposure brings high visibility since some managers are exposed more than others, regardless of their visibility. What constitute exposure and visibility are the subjects' behaviors and the results of their performances. Superiors may be exposed to their subordinates' results without the latter seeing their superiors at all. Or a manager may have visibility to his superiors' behavior and results and not be exposed to them. In many instances, however, exposure and visibility are reciprocal of each other as is traffic on a two-way street. The manager who has visibility may have commensurate exposure.

If a disparity exists, it may be because superiors expose themselves less to subordinates than subordinates do to their superiors. Superiors are responsible for evaluating their subordinates and can invade their domains at will, but subordinates are not called on to evaluate their superiors and must be invited into their territories. Superiors tend to see more of their subordinates and subordinates less of their superiors, which means that managers at all levels usually have greater exposure than visibility. Since superiors have the authority to promote, it is logical that a mobile manager should have more exposure than visibility. It is the amount of exposure and visibility above the normal that is crucial to mobility.

High exposure brings its risks since exposure represents an opportunity to have performances evaluated. Where there is a high potential for positive exposure, there is also an equal opportunity for negative exposure. A mistake, when it is clearly observed, may be more heavily evaluated in a negative manner than when it is only partially seen. Likewise, a successful performance that is clearly observed may be more highly evaluated than when it is partially only observed. Because exposure brings risks and visibility brings only advantages, some managers may value visibility over exposure. They hope to learn from their superiors. Yet if they have little exposure, they may not achieve much mobility. In the world of the mobile manager, zero risk does not exist. The men moving the fastest have highest exposure and learn to live under the high risks that it brings. For this reason, the mobile manager prefers both high exposure and visibility.

Exposure, however, is more difficult to acquire at lower managerial levels while visibility is more difficult to obtain at higher ranks. The reason for this is that the jobs at the top are more crucial and have more inherent exposure automatically. At the lower levels, there are many more managers competing for upward mobility, which makes exposure more difficult to achieve, since an individual manager must stand out from a larger mass. The basic way to become outstanding is to perform crucial assignments upon which superiors' performances are dependent. The lower the position, the less crucial are the manager's performances to others above and below him.

While exposure is more difficult to achieve at lower levels, visibility is less difficult. The reason for this is that there are relatively fewer superiors and many managers sharing their collective impressions of them. The manager at lower levels can usually see superiors better. Visibility is almost given, exposure must be earned.

At this point we must distinguish between lateral exposure and visibility, and vertical. In both instances we shall be talking about superiors and not subordinates or peers. Lateral exposure is represented by superiors who are at the sides of the chain of command under which the manager operates. These lateral superiors may be line or staff people, but they are not in the hierarchy of authority relationships above the manager. Vertical exposure is defined as the number of superiors above the manager who are in the chain of command of which he is one link. The same distinction may be used for lateral and vertical visibility.

Exposure and visibility may be direct and personal or indirect and impersonal. When it is direct, the behavior of the subject is easily observed, and when it is indirect only the results of the subject's performance may be known. Direct visibility is more important than indirect because it allows mobile managers to model their performance from their superiors' behaviors. Indirect exposure, however, offers as many or more advantages to the mobile manager as does direct exposure. Sometimes it is better that results be exposed and not day-to-day behavior, because at times the latter may be embarrassing and marginal. Mobile managers believe it is better that superiors see their results and only a little of their behavior. The penalty is great for over-exposure, but a surplus of direct visibility never hurt any manager. Exposure and visibility that include several levels of superiors are, of course, preferred. Multi-level visibility allows a perspective to evaluate the behavior of an immediate superior. Sometimes immediate superiors lose their objectivity towards subordinates while superiors two levels above and higher may be more objective. Because of this possibility, many corporations require two levels of superiors to decide on promotions, and under this circumstance, multi-level exposure augers well for mobility.

Generally, lateral exposure and visibility come from lateral mobility. The more the manager moves around as he moves up, the better are his chances of getting lateral exposure and visibility. This is why mobile managers value lateral transfers.

Vertical exposure and visibility are largely dependent upon the type of chain of command, the nature of the manager's assignments, the priority of his position, and the mobility of his superiors. If the chain of command above him is formal and autocratic, he may have low exposure and visibility. Superiors will deal directly with their subordinates. At any given level, the superior will see only his subordinate and the subordinate will see only his superior. The ideal is to be exposed to several levels of superiors and to have visibility of them. This situation occurs most often when the chain of command is not formally apparent—when superiors are open, informal, and move freely among people several levels above and below them. The less formal the chain of command, the more multi-vertical will be exposure and visibility.

This leads to a second consideration. Managers may be given assignments that expose them to several levels of superiors. Many staff assignments and special projects may achieve multi-level vertical exposure. Of course, the same assignments and projects may also achieve a high degree of multi-level lateral exposure and visibility. Mobile managers want these types of tasks that yield high lateral and vertical exposure and visibility simultaneously. Few managers who achieve high upward mobility have not had these types of tasks.

In any organization, some functions, departments, and divisions have high priority. These may be high profit centers, high push or rush projects, strategical or tactical assignments. Men in these activities have more exposure and visibility. But we should again caution the reader by noting that the opportunity for high negative exposure is greatest when the opportunity for positive exposure is also greatest.

The more mobile the superior, the more opportunity for the manager to have high exposure and high visibility. As superiors come and go frequently, the manager's opportunity for gaining perspective and handling different types of superiors increases. Furthermore, the more the manager is exposed to numerous superiors, the better are his chances of becoming attached to one and moving with him. Managers who want mobility never despair at the frequent changing of the guard. Only managers who are afraid of exposure feel insecure about the high rate of mobility among superiors. These managers enjoy superiors who stay for a while but unfortunately, superiors who stay in positions for long periods of time are not valid models and mobile subordinates cannot rely upon them for advice and representative opinion and sponsorship. The worst thing that can happen to a mobile manager is to get stuck with an immobile superior.

Contrary to the beliefs of many immobile managers, the best thing for them is to be subject to mobile superiors. With high mobility, a subordinate can be "out" one day and "in" the next, simply because of the departing and arriving of superiors. The reason for an immobile manager's resentment of the frequent changing of superiors is that he must start all over again each time. As one manager put it, "I have broken in three bosses in five years, and I refuse to break another in." It is questionable as to what was "broken in"—his well protected set of defects or the shield of equanimity of his superior. In any case, this manager was not picked up and sponsored by a superior because he never had the confidence in himself and in his superiors to show his best. He hid his talents by presenting to each new superior the same posture of subtle antagonism—hardly a way to become a mobile subordinate.

In the long range view, managers would rather have more lateral exposure and visibility and less vertical since high vertical exposure brings high risk. When a manager who has lateral exposure makes a mistake, he has a chance to try for a position under a superior away from his chain of command. A lateral superior does not usually have as much information about his mistakes and, being more objective, is willing to give him a better chance to recover than his immediate superior was. Lateral exposure represents valuable contacts.

In the short range view, high vertical exposure and visibility are preferred. The reason is that promotions are made on a short range basis and more often than not are made on the basis of whether the manager can handle an assignment that is directly in front of him. When forced to make a choice, the mobile manager will seek high vertical exposure and visibility and gratefully take whatever lateral exposure and visibility may come his way. Although some positive lateral exposure will offset some negative vertical exposure, no amount of positive lateral exposure can bring immediate upward mobility as fast as positive vertical exposure. In the long run, the relative positions of these two factors tend to be reversed.

In short, the compounding of *visibility* and *exposure* into the new mobilographic term *visiposure* is not merely an idle combination of words. With some exceptions, visibility and exposure are reciprocals of each other, exposure brings visibility and visibility brings exposure. Visibility allows the manager to behave like a superior before he is promoted. In the mobile world, promotions are usually after the fact. Before the manager is promoted, he has talked and behaved as one who belongs at a higher level. He appears so much like his superiors that they formalize the relationship. Exposure allows him to gain this advantage. As he sees how they behave, exposure allows him to display his adroitness and mastery. Without exposure, he cannot receive his grades; without visibility he may not learn what the course is really about. Visiposure is an index of the extent to which he has learned his lessons and received honorable grades. Visiposure contributes to and is a consequence of mobility.

Sponsorship

Another factor upon which mobility is dependent is sponsorship, which in turn is dependent upon visiposure. Visiposure is a necessary but not a sufficient condition of sponsorship. To understand the key idea of sponsorship, we must set forth four sets of superiors.

The first set are known as evaluators. They are all superiors, lateral and vertical, who have the necessary visibility to evaluate the manager's performance. The principle is that the broader the base of evaluators, the better the chance of mobility, lateral and upward. To get this broad base of evaluators, the manager must move laterally as he moves up. His position must carry many project assignments and task force assignments that call for working with peers, subordinates, and superiors in many areas outside of his chain of command. A manager may not know all his evaluators but they may be able to know him or his results without his knowing them. We have mentioned this possibility when we said that exposure and visibility may not be equal. Because the mobile manager never knows who his evaluators are, he must always act as though each superior may be evaluating him.

The second set of superiors are known as nominators. They are evaluators who stand well enough with their peers and superiors to be asked to nominate men for promotions. Not all evaluators are nominators and generally only a few superiors are viewed as being blessed with the rare capacity to spot promising and promotable talent. Many managers do not stand well enough even to nominate their successors but those who excel at developing highly talented subordinates are more apt to have nominating power. Managers who stand well with their superiors and with superiors and peers in positions lateral to them are also apt to have nominating powers.

The higher placed executives usually have nominating powers. Even so, there are some who have this capacity to a greater degree than others. Powers of nomination are achieved and are usually a sign of the individual's standing with his lateral and vertical superiors. They are sources of much pride and men feel gratified by being "in" on promotions as a basic psychic reward. But more importantly, powers of nomination are important sources of influence. When a manager has these powers, he can help to determine the managerial mix of the organization without being visibly known. They can be utilized to dispense patronage and ensure the building of a secure base of support below and to the side of the manager. Powers of nomination help to create a supportive environment for the manager.

Yet, powers of nomination are fickle. They can be lost by

merely picking a loser. Managers who are "in" on promotion decisions are very careful not to abuse or misuse their powers. To be certain of their choices, the nominators must have visibility of the men who are eligible for promotions. They must have wide lateral and downward visibility of managers at the side and below. If a superior has been moved laterally frequently, he may have the wide visibility necessary to spot new talent. His nominating powers are greatly enhanced the more he knows the rising young men in positions lateral to him. It is true that a manager who can spot a rare find in some nook or cranny of the corporation has his powers of nomination increased geometrically. But he must not be wrong. His powers of nomination decrease in direct relationship to the magnitude of the errors of his nominee. All of which suggests that the greater his powers of nomination, the more reluctant he is to use them. It is the young, experienced manager who is quick to nominate and to regret later.

The power of nomination is precariously based upon understanding clearly the expectation of superiors. Managers who have visibility to superiors can assess the qualities that they look for in promotees. If the nominator does not know these expectations, he will select men who are not acceptable. Powers of nomination may decrease in direct relationship to the number of nominees who are not acceptable. The mobile manager is more apt not to recommend if he is unsure of what is acceptable. One way to gain this vital information is to listen attentively to the formal and informal remarks that essentially approve of or reject managers' performances. Another way is to watch the men who are promoted for the clues as to their success. The direct approach is to ask the superior what his requirements for the position are. Managers who have retained their powers of nomination never give a recommendation blindly. It is better to ask for information even if the request is resented than to receive a rejection to a nomination. Superiors will forget the probing questions if the choice proves to be good, but will never forget the recommendation that was rejected. A rejection is an indication to the superior that the manager is not aware of what is going on. Such an impression detracts from his future opportunity to nominate.

The third set of superiors are known as sponsors. They are nominators who are different in one major respect. They stand so well with the authority set that the latter will think twice before the sponsors' recommendations are rejected. This seldom happens and in fact, their recommendations are taken so seriously that they are not solicited in an aura of doubt. Notice that the word solicited is used here rather than asked for or demanded. The lower the manager or the fewer his powers of nomination, the more his recommendations will be demanded. The sponsor does not have to offer his wisdom, but when offered, it cannot be gracefully rejected. The principle is that the sponsor will not give advice if it is not properly solicited, if it will not be followed explicitly, and if he cannot be certain of his source of information. When his recommendations are given, they are couched in language that is suggestive and permissive. The recipient is made to feel that he is free to accept or reject it, but, in reality, he does not dare reject it. The recipient receives the command as though it were gratuitous advice. Although this gives him face, he is stuck with the nominee, whether he likes it or not.

The managers and executives who have this critical power of sponsorship are few. Unlike nominators, sponsors may be utilized by their superiors, peers, and subordinates in lateral and vertical positions. The real test of sponsorship is the number of people outside of the sponsor's chain of command who are promoted.

The fourth set of superiors are known as promoters. They are the managers and executives who have the authority to place people. Evaluators, nominators, and sponsors do not have the formal responsibility to select and promote, except in their own areas of authority. The higher placed executive relies upon sponsors and nominators to help him make his decisions. Few promotions occur at levels above middle management without careful examination of the views of nominators and sponsors who may be any place in the corporation. Of course, advice of the latter may be used in ways other than the actual soliciting of their nominations. That is to say, sponsors may be asked to identify critical skills and experiences that serve as a basis of selection. The next step may be to gain information from a broad base of evaluators. Gradually, nominators are plugged into the process and, finally, sponsors may be asked whenever it is proper and necessary to do so. The latter may be asked to confirm a decision, but only when it is understood that they already concur.

A manager may have the authority to promote in his own area or department, but to his superior he may simply be an evaluator of managers who are peers to him. Not all promoters serve as evaluators, nominators, or sponsors to superiors in lateral and vertical positions. When a manager is delegated the authority to promote, he enters the first stage of this process that may lead to his some day becoming a prestigious sponsor. As one who must promote people within his chain of command, he learns the tricky skill of spotting talent and performance. As he excels in his own department, he becomes recognized as a source of evaluations and nominations to other managers above and at his side. With each successive round of success, he grows in stature, but the leap to sponsorship is the largest of all. To become a sponsor, the manager must have a tremendous performance reputation; he must himself excel in managerial skill. So valued is his reputation and skill that his presence cannot be avoided. His reputation for high performance and his skill for nominating winners combine to give him a formidable appearance. His power to influence promotions is far greater than his authority to promote. In this sense he is basically a sponsor and, secondly, a promoter. The sponsor is all four types of superiors wrapped into one man.

The selection and placing of highly positioned managers is a rather lengthy and exhaustive process that is not taken lightly by any one of these four types of superiors. The care with which promotions are made is easily demonstrated in the resulting gain. In the corporate drama of managerial activity, the scenes of evaluation, nomination, sponsorship, and promotion unfold, revealing managers here and there in formal and informal situations. It is a never ending process that consumes vast amounts of time and energy of great numbers of managers. It offers opportunity for many and bestows status upon a few. To be included in the selection and placement process offers a central challenge to the mobile manager.

In conclusion, each day the race to the top produces new winners and losers. The men who win are high performers, but so are many of the men they leave behind. Mobility, like many kinds of success, is based upon being in the right spot at the right time, but arriving there is more skill than luck. In mobilographic terms, it is achieving high visiposure. Constant effort is expended daily in the large corporation without being seen by the right people or evaluated negatively or positively. The corporation is a vast communication medium in which information competes with information in an endless array of variety and with varying degrees of intensity. In this medium, everybody fights against being bowled over by excessive information. Managers at all levels have screening devices based upon priorities that identify relevant information and filter out the mass of irrelevant information. If we consider each manager an information source and receiver, then some managers know better than others how to send and screen information. They achieve penetration of the screens that superiors have to protect against information saturation. Managers become exposed, and once exposed they maintain their priority over others with their superiors. By skill and deft maneuvering they may become sponsors. The mobile manager knows not only how to draw successfully the attention of superiors, but also how to screen the information that superiors release in their behavior and results. He treats with greater priority the information given off by men with powers of nomination and sponsorship. We have seen that mobility is arriving at the right spot at the right time. Next we shall see how mobility is making the best use of this opportunity.

Chapter III

THE CRUCIAL SUBORDINATE

It has often been said that no man is sufficient unto himself. This is particularly true in contemporary society in which technology, science, and the division of labor have effected a precise form of interdependency among people, associations, and institutions. Ours is an organized society in which the manager is emerging as the vital center. In his new role, he has become the manager of laboratory scientists, of college populations, of economic enterprises, and of governmental agencies to name a few of his many functions. As his role in society becomes more dominant, the opportunity to apply and to innovate new skills of managing is steadily increasing.

In large industrial organizations, radically novel ways of managing have emerged in the last two decades. The manager is in the midst of a renaissance in which old ideas are being thrashed over and new ones are being given unusual status. We see this most dramatically in the styles of mobile managers. For them the rite of passage to higher levels is uniformly based upon the desire and ability to change, improve, and experiment. Corporations are increasingly choosing what are often called "wild ducks," managers with a flair for the unique who have the courage and manners to acquire support from others and set the pace for others. The innovative manager stands isolated from those who approach their jobs in a perfunctory manner.

But he is not an island separate from the mainland, he is the mainland, the vital center of the corporation upon which the corporation pivots and achieves its essential character and direction. It is rather the unimaginative, work-oriented manager who is the island apart from the stream of vital activity. The innovative manager is firmly attached to others without whom he could not acquire the opportunity to be different. These "others" are men about him who rely upon his unique skills and talents and he upon theirs. Together they represent a division of skills that maximizes their collective contributions to the firm. The "wild duck" is wild only in his unique talents, not in his ability to coordinate with a group. The mobile manager cannot stand by himself for the value of his skills is predicated upon their usefulness to others. He is crucial to others and, in this sense, he is a central force in his organization and in an organized society.

Managerial mobility is largely a relationship to superiors. Behind every mobile executive is at least one crucial subordinate and often two or three. A crucial subordinate is viewed by his superior to be crucial to his managerial effectiveness. A mobile manager may have twenty or thirty subordinates reporting to him, but he has only one or two crucial subordinates. They are crucial to him because he needs them about as much as or more than they need him. They support him and he, in turn, reports their performances favorably to his superiors. The route to the top is by becoming a crucial subordinate to a mobile superior, by keeping the superior mobile, and by getting out from under him if his upward mobility becomes permanently arrested. This last must be done with care, for the upward mobile manager cannot offend his immobilized superior, who cannot help him, but who can hurt him. After all, the upward bound manager may need him on the way down.

The crucial subordinate gains when his superior has the status of a sponsor, who can offer the subordinate protection. Sometimes what is a crucial skill at one level, however, is not at a higher level. If the subordinate loses his cruciality, his superior, who has the capacity to sponsor, may find a position for him in a lateral area in the firm that holds high visiposure and potential mobility. No one ever gets hurt by becoming a crucial subordinate unless he greatly disappoints the superior. He must take the high risk that accompanies high exposure.

There are two kinds of crucial subordinate—supplementary and complementary. A supplementary crucial subordinate (SCS) tends to add to his superior's strengths and acts largely like his superior, in contrast to the complementary crucial subordinate (CCS) who tends to fill in his superior's deficiencies and to overcome his weaknesses. For example, an executive who cannot communicate easily has as his crucial subordinate (CCS) a good communicator. Although many superiors apparently still look for themselves in their subordinates (SCS types), the trend is definitely toward the complementary type of crucial subordinate.

The most mobile manager is a complementary crucial subordinate for two reasons. First, the assignments at the executive level require a complement of skills and, second, two or three persons who are in a complementary relationship can make a bigger indentation on the corporation than the same number in a supplementary relationship. Complementary teams have larger visiposure, as do their individual members.

To find and develop complementary crucial subordinates successfully requires a knowledge of weaknesses and strengths. Some managers are incapable of frankly assessing their own weaknesses. By discovering these and having subordinates cover them, the executive becomes a formidable manager. His mobility is better assured as is that of his crucial subordinates.

Crucial subordinates are seldom recognizable by their titles, authority, salaries, or job descriptions. There is only one reliable way to spot them—by the company they keep. A superior moves up and takes one or two people with him. In the period before the 1950's, a superior would move and a year or so later call for his subordinates. Today superiors move their subordinates along in simultaneous sequence or place them in positions that they have vacated. The reason for this is apparent. If a superior is going to stay in his new position for only a couple of years, he is unwilling to waste a year of talent utilization.

Another possible way to spot crucial subordinates is in the way their mistakes are evaluated. It is foolish to suppose that men who move to the top do not make mistakes. The pertinent fact is the manner in which their mistakes are evaluated. A crucial subordinate has his mistakes underevaluated. Perhaps publicly his superiors overevaluate these mistakes in order not to show favoritism, but privately they minimize them to a certain extent. The reason is that mobile superiors do not like to believe that they have made bad choices and they may need the crucial subordinates as badly as the latter need their superiors. Many times men have made mistakes of major proportions but their total performance has been evaluated without full reference to these. We can now say that few men arrive at the top who have made no major managerial errors. But what is an error? It is not a fact, but rather a judgment about a fact. Sponsors always color their evaluations of the acts of their crucial subordinates—a tendency which can place the managers in a difficult position if it is carried to excess. Mobile managers are not in the final analysis as concerned with their subordinates' mistakes as with their superiors' evaluations.

Another possible way to detect a crucial subordinate is by the greater amount of freedom and resources granted to him so that he can perform his job well. Mobility is a game of double or nothing. Managers who perform well achieve mobility and those who have reputations for rising talent are given more opportunity to perform highly. Performance and mobility relate geometrically to give a total greater than the sum of the parts, a phenomenon called potentiation, which accounts for the rapid upward mobility of a shooting star type.

We have alluded to the fact that a crucial subordinate is evaluated as a high performer. But high performance in itself does not predict upward mobility. There are more high performers than upward mobiles. If achieving objectives and investing hard energy in work were the basis of upward mobility, there would be more at the top than at the bottom. The future president leaves behind many hard workers each time he is promoted. The fact of the matter is that high performance as it is variously defined is a necessary but not a sufficient cause of upward mobility.

One sufficient cause is trust. As we said in Chapter I, few men arrive at the top who are not trusted by someone already there, nor are few men placed in crucial positions at any level who are not trusted by their superiors. A crucial position can be defined as one that could affect the career of the superior. Trust is a difficult term to define. The manager can sense that another does not trust him, but he does not know exactly the cause of the distrust. He may find reasons to justify his suspicions. Similarly the same manager may not trust another and not know exactly why. Yet, as irrational and emotional as is this factor of trust, it has tremendous career-pulling power, and is an outstanding quality of the men at the top.

High performance and trustworthiness describe the characteristics of the crucial subordinate. We must next define career point. Many executives look back on their pasts and see points in their career when they had everything operating in their favor but missed their opportunity. They had the right kind of superior and the kind of work that could reveal their best skills and motives. This situation constitutes a career point and only about four or five of them occur in the life of a mobile manager. At these points many managers fail to achieve a condition of trust with their superiors because of the violation of any one of the four conditions of trust—accessibility, availability, predictability, and loyalty.

The first is accessibility. The accessible manager is one

who takes in ideas easily and gives them out freely. Think of a friend and you will see a man who values your ideas. He may ultimately disagree, but he will first roll the idea around in his mind and give it a chance to appear worthy. The opposite of accessible mind is a closed mind. The subordinate who thinks more highly of his own ideas than those of his superiors never receives trust. His closed mind is also seen in his unwillingness to share his ideas and information with others. One can always sense when someone is holding out; he is suspect, his motives are evaluated as selfish when in fact he may be rather shy.

It must be stated that the crucial subordinate does not necessarily always agree with his superior. The minimum requirement of trust in this sense is that the subordinate respects new and different ideas enough to think them through carefully and energetically. Screening them out after careful deliberation enhances the creativity of both superior and subordinate. Mutual respect will grow from the necessity to disagree because of the overpowering force of cold logic. Radical disagreement may exist between the two, but it is never over the legitimacy of new ideas and the sincerity of the subordinate.

The second condition of trust is availability. The principle is that the manager who thinks more highly of his own job than of his superior's does not receive trust. A good illustration of this comes from a personal experience. An executive declined the customary invitation to lunch with the author during a day-long interview because the president of the corporation was in a difficult board of director's meeting. The author inquired if the president had asked the executive to stay in case he was needed. The executive said that this was not the case but that he had learned to be available at certain times in case his superior sent down for information or suggestions. He said that he had learned that it was wise to anticipate his superior who had come to rely upon him. This executive was a trailer as far back as when he was a production supervisor and the president was plant manager.

It is an unwritten rule that managers should be attentive to their superiors. A superior should never have to be the first to inform a subordinate of the former's problem. A perceptive subordinate should be able to put clues together and not be taken by surprise. The superior who can rely upon a subordinate to be alert and informed will not always have to start his briefing from scratch. A crucial subordinate has a wide span of attention that allows him to attend to many problems beyond those that confront him directly.

There are some managers who cannot monitor their superiors. Their cognitive facilities are not developed enough to attend to two activities at the same time. There are other managers who operate under the mistaken assumption that if their superior needs them, he will let them know. The manager who in using good judgment makes himself available to the superior's needs and problems at the strategically proper time comes a long way toward meeting the condition of trust.

Of course, the manager must be careful not to reveal an overzealous attitude of wanting to move into the superior's territory or of usurping his authority. One of the unspoken expectations that superiors have of subordinates is the prevention of major mistakes if it is within the province of the subordinates to do so. The manager has absolutely no defense if he fails to correct the superior when the latter suspects that the former had information better than his own. The subordinate may plead that his advice was not asked for, but his failure to protect his superior will certainly not auger trust. The crucial subordinate serves as his superior's third eye and third ear and never assumes that all of his needs will be made explicit.

The third condition of trust is predictability. This word does not refer to being able to predict the daily habits and hours of a subordinate. Predictability means that the subordinate will handle delicate administrative circumstances with good judgment and thoroughness. An illustration of predictability is the case of a chairman of the board of directors whose crucial subordinate, the president, was not at the board meeting to defend himself. An outside board member asked why the president had made a particular decision. The chairman's reply was essentially that the president made decisions based on facts, and that when the facts of this particular case were known, the reasons for the decision would be clear. Predictability means the assumption that the president would always make his decisions based upon fact and even though his superior might look at the same facts and arrive at a different decision, the superior could defend the decision to his authorities because it was based upon facts. The minimum condition of trust in the sense of predictability is that the superior can defend and justify a decision and he is confident that this will always be possible.

The last condition of trust is loyalty—personal loyalty. Organization loyalty may be important, but it does not carry the career-pulling power of personal loyalty. Mobile executives and managers never entrust a crucial responsibility to a subordinate who they suspect will sacrifice them for selfish gain or for abstract "principles." Principles that cause superiors to be sacrificed may serve the conscience of a subordinate, but hardly the career plans of a superior. The manager lives in an eminently human world; if he is smart, he will treat his superior as a human first and a manager second. That is to say that one *can* follow principle and go to the top of the corporation as long as one remembers that there is a vast difference between a manager who will readily expose his superior's errors and one who will reluctantly do so only after it becomes clear that others will not personally benefit by such disclosures.

To a large extent, a crucial subordinate fulfills all four conditions of trust: accessibility, availability, predictability and loyalty. These conditions are severe and exert a dominant influence upon the nature of the superior-subordinate relationship. Trust operates most acutely at levels where the responsibilities are more encompassing and critical to the executive career, but it operates to a certain extent at all managerial levels.

Trust is a vital condition where control of the behavior of the manager is minimal. If the superior could control the subordinate's behavior completely, he would not have to rely upon trust. Managers who cannot trust others usually attempt to overcontrol them. They substitute control for trust.

But most executives find great advantage in giving subordinates wide latitude and they derive great gains from the creativity that usually ensues. This cannot be done for all subordinates or they might misuse their freedom, but controls will be minimized when there is opportunity to invest trust. The more the manager is trusted, the more opportunity he has to make decisions based upon his own choices. The more opportunity he has to develop his powers of self-expression, the better the chance of bringing fresh and unique approaches to his work and that of his superiors.

We have noted in the first chapter that men who move to the top have reputations. They have become known because they have done things differently and have kept their superior's support. This was possible largely because their superiors trusted them. Perhaps it will always be easier to appear and act bright when the environment is supportive. In any case, trust must be earned and the degree of trust that binds a superior and his crucial subordinate is the rare blending of compatible drives and emotions of two or more people who need and support each other. Together they can do more than the same number of people whose solidarity is more formal or mechanical than organic or functional.

Crucial subordinates have sponsorship but not of the protégé type. A sponsor-protégé relationship usually exists between a subordinate and a superior many levels above, who may offer his patronage to his subordinate through the levels to the top. The essential difference between the crucial subordinate and the sponsor-protégé is that there is no functional or organic relationship between the latter pair. It is possible that the sponsor-protégé may come to work so closely together that their skills intermesh. At this point, the pair becomes a superior-crucial subordinate. In only a few cases does the sponsor-protégé relationship ever become translated into a crucial subordinate relationship. Many mobile managers become at various times in their career patterns protégés of some highly positioned superior. More often they move up because they are crucial subordinates to mobile superiors.

To become a protégé, the manager must have tremendous amounts of exposure. A minimum amount of visibility is necessary because the subordinate does not discover the sponsor. With the crucial subordinate the reverse is true. To become a crucial subordinate a minimum amount of exposure is required, but of the kind which gains the attention of the immediate superior. This exposure to the superior must be intensive. The manager's visibility of the superior must also be intensive. Visiposure allows both superior and subordinate the necessary information to fulfill the four conditions of trust. Without intensive visiposure, crucial subordination is not possible. Visiposure is the necessary condition for crucial subordination which, in turn, is the necessary condition for mobility. The condition that will guarantee mobility to a crucial subordinate is for the superior to be highly mobile himself. This means that he will undoubtedly be a crucial subordinate to his superior.

It is not uncommon to see a chain of crucial subordinates encompassing several levels of management. If the top man has his upward mobility arrested, the lower managers may telescope into each other. This condition is sometimes more real than humorous. A senior executive was fired from the corporation and the three levels of subordinates had their careers jeopardized. The problem of the crucial subordinate is that he may go the way of his superior. To prevent this, the mobile manager attempts not to identify openly and publicly with the superior. If the superior has the good of his crucial subordinate at heart, he will not allow overidentification to occur. For this reason, crucial subordinates are not easily spotted. The only sure way is by the tendency for them to move with their superiors.

Chapter IV

THE STYLE OF THE MOBILE MANAGER

Each manager applies to his responsibilities a style that is peculiar to himself. Even where the position is well established, the manager will reveal a style that is different from that of any previous manager. Style is basically a fine balance between the manager's perception of the job, and his manner of carrying it out. Since all managers are basically different and perceive differently, styles are without duplication.

The style of a mobile manager takes account of the fact and requirements of mobility. He uses prudently a rear view mirror that tells him what he has done successfully and a telescope that predicts what he must do today to prepare for the future. At any given time he is addressing himself to the past, present, and future. He thinks and acts in triple time. He utilizes this tri-focal orientation for personal gain. To him the past that is meaningful is found in his present skills and the future that is hoped for prepares him to meet his present opportunities. The mobile manager commandeers time for the purpose of enhancing his great desire to achieve. In this sense, we may say that the mobile manager excels in his management of time.

We shall see that some positions clearly compress experience and require efficient management of time. Some of these positions carry projects and special assignments and have time limitations for the execution of objectives. We shall also see that the requirements of time management force the manager to enter and leave a job in ways different from those of the previous generation of managers. He must have a mobile style of managing.

Project Manager

One important type of mobile manager is the project manager. Before the decades of the fifties and sixties, presidents were given the reins to hold as long as they could drive the team through the muddy field of economic competition. They stayed in command as long as ten to fifteen years, with no terminal point arbitrarily set by the corporate officials. Today, presidents stay in about five years and are project types. These men are asked to do a particular job, to accomplish a particular set of objectives, after which they turn the baton over to the next team of executives in the relay race.

Executives become presidents because corporate situations require their particular talents. Long range planning has produced a kind of rhythm that determines movement of people to the top in specialized groups. There are project dyads and triads. A president and a chairman may move into and out of their respective offices together. The fact is that a corporation does not promote an executive to the presidency. An executive with a team of three or four moves into the command structure at the top. Completing corporate plans calls for a sensitive blending of skills that must take account of the unique features of the corporate situation. Because of the increasingly technical nature of corporate activity, project type assignments are creeping down to middle management levels. To execute project assignments successfully, the manager must know how to organize teams of limited purposes and at times to draw talent from the far corners of the company. As a project manager, he must motivate people who have their loyalties attached to other superiors and functions. After the project is completed, the team will disband and its members return to their former assignments or get new ones. The nature of business today requires an endless array of projects that call upon specialized talent from all over the corporation. So common are projects today that few men arrive at the top without having served in them many times.

Project managers and members of project teams gain high degrees of visiposure of the lateral and vertical types. Oftentimes authority differences are collapsed during the period of the project and team members of varying degrees of superiority may function as equals. There is no substitute for the visiposure that comes from project assignments. Because visiposure is increased greatly by project assignments, the opportunity for crucial subordination is equally enhanced.

So common are project assignments that the concept of position is losing its usefulness. The generation that preceded the mobile manager was assigned work that belonged to an area or office identified on the organization chart as a position. It was a formal description of work duties that varied little with the managers who moved into the position. If a manager had his work duties increased, they were increased permanently for all subsequent managers. With the advent of project assignments, a position became more of a skeleton of minimum duties. Positions became less descriptive of what the manager was required to do because the manager was constantly flooded with projects of all kinds. Today, the greater part of managerial development is found in project performance rather than in position managing. To put it differently, management by objective surpassed in career value the performance of duties. We can see this most aptly in outspan positions.

Outspan Positions

This term is derived from the practice of unyoking work animals at the end of an exhausting day of labor. In many corporations there are positions in which the stresses are so great that executives cannot be left in them longer than two years before they need the "outspan" or rest. Normally, the higher placed executives stay in their positions longer than mobile middle managers. The exception to this fact is the executive in the stress position. For him, two years is the average relative time which compares favorably with that of mobile middle managers.

Before the mid-century, the concept of outspan was not widely known. What gave it widespread recognition was the fact of rapid corporate growth. During this period, priorities were assigned to functions or divisions and limited objectives were established to be met in a relatively short period of time. Managers arrived and departed, each of whom attempted to execute different limited objectives. Those who did well under the pressure were often moved to another job of equal or more stress. In the second or third job of this kind, good men were often ruined. It became apparent that a sequence of stressful positions had to be spliced by positions that were relatively routine by comparison. At first the manager completing a stress assignment was lateraled to an outspan position for the purposes of giving him a rest and of saving him for another critical job in the near future. Managers soon discovered that the relatively easy and slow work in the outspan assignments afforded them an opportunity to gain perspective about what they had learned in the stress job. They soon grew impatient in the outspan assignment and their desire was renewed to get back into the stream of stress again. The outspan positions, however, gave them the vital resources of insight and added drive, which can be lost from severe amounts of unbroken stress.

Managers who stayed in the stream of stress too long showed a pattern which we may identify as stress reaction. It is most commonly found among men who have executed several sets of objectives in the same stress position or have been in three or more stress positions without relief. An early symptom is an inability to tolerate anything that is relatively routine and slow. One day of vacation and the manager is ready to go back to work. He may be unwilling even to consider a vacation. He has a strong tendency to withdraw from any problem that requires careful, meticulous thought and inquiry, a preoccupation with minor aspects of that part of the job that is crucial, a tendency to freeze the nature of problems at that point where they were first identified. As one executive undergoing stress reaction said to a staff member, "For god's sake, don't find any more problems than we have now. We've got our hands full as it is." A later symptom of stress reaction is an inability to react at all to stressful events. Conditioned to handle stress, he is unable to get his adrenalin moving at all. He appears almost apathetic. Actually, he becomes careless about critical objectives, treating them as routine and common. When he should spring into total and personal involvement, he relies upon second-hand evidence. His actions become partial and ill timed. He may sense that he is not reacting as he should and tells himself that tomorrow or the next day he will really sail into the job as he had done many times before. But the zip is gone, and in some cases it may never be retrieved again. The author has seen managers burned out as early as their middle forties because they were not relieved at strategic times. Corporations are much the wiser today about the relationship between mobility and stress.

It is hard to control the levels of stress. If a mobile manager is put into a position that has become widely recognized as a stress type, he knows that he has to accomplish limited objectives in two years and he will then be relieved. This knowledge and the desire to maintain his reputation as a high performer will not reduce the amount of stress. A man who knows that he must give his all for a short period of time will attempt to give more than he has in him. On the other hand, if he knows he will be in the job four or five years, he will pace himself as though he were in a cross-country track event. Too often he approaches his stress position much as though he were running a hundred year dash. This factor of self-induced stress may become as great as the stress inherent in the job itself. The problem is that his superiors have little control over the amount of stress that he may self-induce. They may warn him not to overreact, but he knows that if he fails in the job, he alone will be held responsible. What his superiors can control is his next job assignment, and if they are wise, they will move him out of the stress stream. He knows, however, that they will do this whether he succeeds in the job or fails. The only thing he can do is to throw his whole self into the job, and the fear that even this is not enough may force him to exceed the limits of his ability and energy. This may solve his short range problem but create a long range one. If he cannot apply good judgment in a stress job, what evidence is there that he will make the best use of the outspan—his opportunity to rest and refresh himself.

The advantage of a stress assignment followed by an outspan is found in their geometrical relationship; the one helps the manager discover his potential; the other helps to keep it available to the corporation. The corporation is always in need of identifying the manager who can perform in critical positions and the manager's potential to do so cannot be fully assessed unless he tries his hand at a high stress position. The yields are so great, aside from those gained by achieving the objective of the job itself, that one cannot imagine a corporation that does not make instrumental use of stress-outspan positions.

Developmental Positions

Ideally, every position is developmental in that each calls forth previously acquired skills and experiences and prepares the manager for more responsible assignments. We may say that each position calls for a unique ordering of skills and experiences. Unfortunately, some managers override the unique features of a position by maintaining a style that was useful in previous positions, ignoring the differences that inhere in the new position. Managers have been known to move through several different positions without varying their managerial styles as though they had learned nothing new. What has happened is that they have frozen the process of development to a level of high initial effectiveness. They have set their styles and they force position responsibilities to comply with them. Regardless of the number of positions they have held, they have in effect managed the same position several times, repeating the same experiences again and again. Style rigidity can set in easily because managing is not a fine art. There are wide tolerances of success and failure that allow for rather gross and imprecise levels of skill and development. A common saying is that a poor decision can be made to work if it is believed in. This is true of a poor managerial style that is aggressively applied.

When mobility exceeds development, the manager often repeats the same mistakes, carrying with him from job to job the same problems. He may even have a set procedure for handling the problem, but it is more remedial than preventive. He has learned how to minimize his difficulties. Such an oblique approach starves the manager of preventive experience and will arrest his upward mobility at levels where the tolerances that cover his problem are narrow. A manager never knows exactly when a remedial solution may become a problem itself. This is the case when a short range solution becomes a long range problem. The manager who is interested in sustaining his mobility will attempt to alter his style to account for the unique features of each new position. He makes full use of his development opportunities since to him, each position is a developmental one.

Every position calls for new skills in addition to ordering a unique arrangement of previously acquired skills and experiences. If the new skills that are required are radically different from those previously acquired, the manager faces a developmental gap. This may occur for several reasons. The first, of course, is the failure to learn from previous jobs. If we assume that he has cranked out from his previous positions all the possible skills, the second reason may be that the new position is inherently too advanced for his level of development. He may have been promoted too fast. Perhaps his sponsor made an error in judgment; he misjudged either the manager or the new position, or both. Such mismatches occur frequently, and unfortunately the manager will carry the blame for the failure that may ensue.

A third reason for a developmental gap is that the manager did not stay long enough in his previous positions to really master them. During the last decade, some managers have moved faster than they have been able to absorb their experiences, or managers may not have stayed long enough to have had their performances evaluated. Mistakes from which managers learn the most are those that are not identified for as long as a year after they have occurred. It takes that long for the repercussions to set in and for evaluations to be made. As one manager said, "If you are going to make mistakes, move faster than they do." This, of course is a dangerous policy.

The developmental gap can become a positive force in that the manager may be forced to tap talent that cannot be reached by any other means. Each manager has potential of which he is unaware. If he meets the crisis successfully, he is a better man in several ways. He knows better what he can do under stress and he has created new potential by transforming potential talent into actual talent. The miracle of learning is that it creates as much potential as it actualizes. Theoretically, the manager is never deprived of potential, but only of the opportunity to actualize it. We may then say that one way to overcome quickly a developmental gap is to throw a manager in over his head and force him to sink or swim. Some learn very fast while others panic. Those that succeed receive an experiential advantage in that they have eliminated the developmental gap, sustained their mobility and acquired a tremendous sense of self-confidence. The possibility is great that in the next job they will find a surplus of skill and confidence. It may take them less time than usual to master the next job and do it easily. In this way they have eliminated the developmental gap.

The mobility gap is an entirely different phenomenon. Here the manager has developed faster than his mobility. What he wants to do to increase his mobility is to take up some of the slack in his development. The chief reason for a mobility gap is that he experiences his positions more efficiently than most. It takes him less time to learn and control the new position and the mobility needed to sustain his developmental curve is not forthcoming. He is "hungry." Every additional day in the position causes his developmental curve to decrease rapidly. The few additional experiences cost him abnormal amounts of career time. The longer he stays immobile, the greater the mobility gap. He is overprepared for the next job because he learned the present one too quickly. In contrast to the manager with a developmental gap who has underlearned his positions, he has overlearned his job.

Overlearning may be caused by not having had exposure to evaluators. Superiors may come to expect a normal learning period that covers most subordinates. The exceptions may be missed, especially if they are obscurely positioned. Overlearning is indeed most apt to occur among managers in positions of the more routine type with low exposure. For various reasons, an efficient learner may be put into one of these routine positions and stay far longer than other managers who learn less efficiently in more exposed positions.

One reason a fast learner may be shunted off into an obscure position is that he is a disturbing fast learner. The superior may want to reduce his exposure simply because he cannot stand his presence. If this is the case, a most logical result usually occurs. The fast learner becomes more irritating as his exposure is reduced because he becomes bored quickly with his new assignment and because he must make a bigger noise to overcome his reduced exposure. Unless the superior realizes the essence of his situation, it may become worse. If the fast learner is given a demotion, his mobility gap will become that much larger.

In larger corporations, there are many managers who have wide mobility gaps. These are men who can perform at higher levels if they are given an opportunity. Management maintains that it is always looking for talent, but what it may not be aware of is that much needed talent lies in the most unexposed places, below executives and managers who cannot stand the irritating qualities that often belong to fast learners.

A superior who has underlearned and a subordinate who has overlearned can make an ideal match. This is true if the superior has not underlearned the skill to handle the fast learner. The problem with some mobile executives is that they move their crucial subordinates too fast because they themselves move too fast. To avoid this double jeopardy, the mobile superior may latch occasionally onto an older, more experienced subordinate. Behind every mobile executive, there is at least one subordinate who is eight to ten years his senior. This matching of energy and ambition with experience and deliberativeness represents a powerful meld, well packed with potential mobility for both.

Arriving, Performing, Departing

Business executives have often been called men of action. They find in their routines and challenges a high sense of achievement and identity. They are what they have done. Their relative worth is a function of the objectives that have been set for them and achieved by them. As fitting as this description was of business executives, it is no longer descriptive of men facing the decade of the seventies. As a group they are fast becoming men whose core of values is centered around mobility. If they value action, it is because it yields advancement and change. The activity they value most is that of mobility itself. For the mobile manager, arriving is departing. However, the challenge is more than this. It is a product of moving into a new job, achieving certain objectives, preparing to move out, and repeating the cycle again and again. If performing satisfactorily gave his predecessor a thrill, moving through several layers of positions and performing each job well increases geometrically the sense of achievement of a mobile manager. For him, executing well the many arrivings and departings is no mean feat. It is as big a task as doing the job itself. Mobile managers maintain that performing the task is inseparable from arriving and departing. They see arriving, performance, departing (APD) as a triad of activities that is performed, each in relationship to the other. The mobile manager executes his task in such a manner as to ensure departing and he arrives in such a manner as to expedite performance. Mobility is more than mere job performance. For instance, mobile managers claim that the best way to get a promotion is to train a good replacement. Graceful departing is essentially executing a smooth transfer of authority. Gaps in work routines and drastic shifts in managerial styles are avoided. The corporation progresses by incremental changes. Unique differences in temperament and skills that inevitably characterize the successor and the predecessor are not allowed to disturb drastically the ebb and flow of organizational activity. It is not that the mobile manager is uninnovative. Nothing could be farther from the truth. Rather, he installs new or different objectives and means in close coordination and sympathy with those of his predecessor. It is not uncommon for a departing manager to chair his staff meeting at ten o'clock with his newly appointed successor at his side, and at eleven o'clock sit at the right hand of a superior whom he is about to replace. When the public is notified that a new president has been appointed or a senior manager elevated to a new post, chances are that the executive has been gradually performing his new responsibilities for three to nine months prior to his formal appointment. At lower levels, this lead time is less.

Successful departing is related to the condition in which the job was found by the new arrival. It does little for the departer's mobility to leave the job in worse condition than when he found it leaving his mistakes for his successor to clean up. Oftentimes he will be asked to nominate his successor. A great part of graceful departing is based upon making a selection and receiving support for his nomination. Managers and executives are evaluated highly for their ability to spot and develop managers. In a mobile world, a good manager is one who can produce managers. The corporation will run out of managers if everyone who is promoted does not train a replacement at least as good as himself or better. The most mobile men are breeders of managerial talent. In short, departing is a basic managerial skill.

The skills of graceful arriving are equally crucial to managing effectively. What constitutes a job is necessarily routine and rudimentary procedures to which previous experiences are directly applicable. Graceful arriving is performed by an exercise called mapping. The entering executive studies intently the expectations of his new superior and those of peers and subordinates and arranges in his mind a priority of objectives that carries relative degrees of value. Even while he is performing his initial set of work assignments, he is mapping to find the few things that count the most. By arranging priorities, he avoids the administration of triviality. Managers are often told by their superiors to "quit handling routine and trivia and start making decisions." Men who hear this admonition have failed to sense the inherent priorities, some of which are not explicitly revealed to them by their superior or immediately apparent to ordinary inspection. Mapping requires a kind of extra perception to the demands of the position other than those immediately apparent. The end of the executive arrival stage occurs when he has mapped the terrain sufficiently to feel confident of his priorities and then proceeds to execute accordingly. He is now in the performance stage of the APD trilogy.

One can always pick out the graceful arrivals by the manner in which they set time aside to map. They know intuitively and experientially that much of what was valued in the previous job is not valued in the new job. If the two value systems were the same, their priorities would necessarily be different. The mobile manager understands that what was important in one job may not be important in another.

The previous generation of managers acted on the principle that what worked in one managerial situation, usually worked in another. For example, all Secretaries of Defense before Robert S. McNamara applied this rule of thumb. They took rules of behavior from law offices and automobile companies and applied them to managing the Pentagon. In one case, the Secretary believed that what was good for his former company was good for the Pentagon. Their successes were indeed few. We may differ about the results of McNamara's regime, but we must admit that he has changed the military establishment in such a way that it will never be the same. His first six months in office were basically a period of mapping. He asked himself what was important to the Army, where were the key forces in the Navy, who were the strong men in the Air Force. Once he had mapped his terrain and ascertained the maze of values, he then proceeded to execute his objectives. His effectiveness is largely due to how well he handled himself during these six months that marked his arrival period. His priorities were extremely sensitive to those of people he had to influence. The crucial problem in the arrival stage is not simply what is important to whom, but when is it important. Hence, the need to be bright about sensing and arranging priorities.

Arriving, performing, and departing represent skills that men of action did not usually acquire as long as they saw mobility related largely to job performance. We have all seen how the first six months in office can set the tone for the whole tenure. First impressions are lasting and replacements can come on too fast for those the manager must influence and control. Newness is to many a threat itself because they have become accustomed to a particular set of values and priorities. New managers who reveal their differences gradually perform better. Mobile managers come on slowly, perform swiftly after achieving rapport, and depart or break gradually and cleanly. This rhythm is characterized as style.

Of course, there are exceptions to this rhythm of arriving, performing, departing. There is an executive whose managerial style is such that he shakes people within the first few months after his entry into a new position. He is commonly called a stinger, and he is most useful when a department or division has settled down comfortably to setting goals and objectives below their potential. The stinger can thoroughly shake up this practice, and if he is followed by a manager with an organizing flair, the department or organization can be reorganized to a new level of performance. There are cases where the inertia of a group cannot be broken any other way. Even the rhythmic style of a mobile manager fails to achieve the effect that a stinger followed by a mobile manager can produce in tandem.

The tandem concept is becoming increasingly common today. It is a product of a mobile organization world. Two men with different managerial styles can more successfully move a staff than any single manager during an equal period of time. Under certain conditions, two men who each stay two years, sharing a common set of objectives and the performance of them, will register a greater degree of success than one man who has been given the same set of objectives to be performed during a tenure of four years.

Of course, the tandem principle does not always bear superior results. Sometimes the inherent quality of the staff or objectives, or the skill of the manager may exert a prohibitive effect. But the gradual increase in the use of the tandem concept suggests that more jobs are amenable to the advantages than were once believed. This is particularly true of the tandem in which the stinger is followed by a manager with a flair for organizing.

The man of action type was depended upon to set an entirely different set of values and priorities upon immediate entrance to a new job. The staff that he inherited was always prepared for the worst. His first day in the job was the barometer of things to come in the future. If things were chaotic, he was expected to correct this situation as soon as possible. The previous generation of managers came on hard and, if successful, they stayed a relatively longer time than do the mobile managers of the new generation. In a mobile organization where bosses come and go within one-half or less of the time of their predecessors, coming on hard elevates the emotions of the staff they inherit. To sustain the advantages of rapid mobility, the rhythmic style of arriving, performing, and departing is fundamental to effective managing.

The principle is clear. A manager can get more done if he plans. The managers who were activists were geared to run and not map, depart and not prepare the ground for the smooth change-over of the guard. The mobile manager is so accustomed to mobility that he is prepared to manage the stages of arriving and departing with as much dexterity as he manages the performance phase. To him, managing is largely mastering the skills of mobility.

Chapter V

THE SHELF SITTER

The great tidal wave of upward mobility has swelled the ranks of men who have had their fondest dreams realized. Our society accords great prestige to the men who occupy the executive suites. This is particularly true of mobile hierarchs who have made it to the top without the help of relationships through family or marriage. The respect for their achievement is directly proportionate to the distance that they have travelled, to the speed of their rise, and most important, to the extent that they have done so independently.

What the public may not fully understand is that this youngest generation of top executives did not defy the law of averages that prevailed before World War II. Relatively more men reside at the top today. The president interacts on a face-to-face basis with at least four times as many executives as he did two decades ago, and his immediate subordinates have more line, staff, and personnel support. In short, men in the arrival stage are more numerous and consequently have had the benefit of a higher mobility rate than any preceding generation of managers.

What may seem to mitigate against this point is that the office of the president is still occupied by a single individual. Because there is only one corporate president at a time while many executives strive for this responsibility, the competition at the top is very intense. Mobility in the office of the presidency has raised the hopes and ambitions of executives far more than it has created the actual opportunity of realizing them. On the other hand, mobility in the presidency has aided to a substantial degree the opportunity to occupy the highest office and other positions in the arrival stage. We can see this mobility factor operating by noting the number of managers and executives who are moved as a consequence of the vacating and filling of a single position at the top. In a large industrial corporation, a partial mobility audit revealed a very high degree of geographical mobility among all levels of managers. In one particular case, a manager had been moved geographically three times in five and a half years. The president thought that this was too much and directed that for one year no more geographical moves could be approved at any level without the highest superior checking with him personally. A week later the executive vice-president died suddenly. To replace him some one hundred moves were eventually recorded that were directly attributable to the death of this top executive. It is ironical that the manager in question was moved once again, making it four times in six years. We can see how increasing the number of executives and decreasing the amount of time spent in their positions has increased the opportunities of managers at all levels to get into the arrival stage. Mobile managers have had many factors operating in their favor during these last two decades.

Competition for mobility has increased at all levels in the corporation, but particularly at the middle management levels. One of the reasons for this is found in the rising expectations of the members of our society in general to be able to improve in education, position and status. The future executive came from World War II better equipped to garner career success. He proved to be a better college student, more skillful in handling people, and more ready to pay whatever costs would be incurred in total success.

Another reason for competition is that the number of managerial employees has increased faster than the number of non-managerial employees. In terms of relative growth rates, the corporation cannot be represented by the usual pyramid. The relative increase in the number of managers (men between entrance and arrival stages, see Chapter I) requires that we describe the corporation by the profile of a light bulb in which the widest part (the girth) represents middle management. Here competition has been greatly intensified. There have always been more managers than executives, but the relative proportion of managers to executives has nearly doubled. This may be accounted for by a number of factors. One is the increased use of automation that has reduced the relative size of the work force and has made economically possible the increase in the number of managers and their salaries. In addition, the number of managers of managers (M.O.M.) has increased because the number of managers that are managed by any one superior has decreased. Project assignments and special task forces of all kinds have reduced the effective span of control. The result has been that at the managers of managers level, more men have failed to maintain their upward mobility. Another way to say this is that relatively more men have made it to middle management and relatively fewer have reached the executive levels above them. We would expect, then, to find a large number of managers who have had their upward mobility arrested. This possibility has been confirmed by the mobilographic studies done thus far.

The passed-over generation is found preponderantly in the second, third, and fourth levels of management. While the public sees the larger number of men who carry the prestigious titles of corporate executives, namely president, executive vice president, group vice president, vice president, assistant to the vice-president, and president of divisions, it does not see the vast number of middle managers, nor does it see the large number who have had their upward mobility arrested and now sit precariously or recline gracefully on corporate shelves. While our economy has produced the largest group of young executives in his-

tory, it has also created the largest number of shelf sitters.

Before we describe shelf sitters and their problems,
we must take account of the phenomenon of channel imbalance and channel blockage. Channel imbalance is a condition where some routes that transport men to the top
acquire more men at a given level in the corporation than
can be promoted to higher positions. For example, in one
corporation, accountants move up rapidly and in high
numbers in positions carrying managerial responsibilities
in finance and accounting, but because few men from the
accounting channel go to the executive level in this corporation, the accounting channel is imbalanced. Balance
would exist if the channel were to transport its per capita
share of men to the top. In this same corporation, managers
at the same levels in engineering processes move up more
slowly and in smaller numbers, but a greater per capita
share of them goes into the top corporate levels. In fact,
there are few officers of the corporation who did not spend
the major share of their middle management careers in
engineering and allied responsibilities.

Another way to discover channel imbalance is by looking
at mobility rates of divisions. In this corporation, a particular division had three times the average number of managers at middle managerial levels than the average number
for all divisions, yet it produced less than one-third of its
per capita share of executives.

In addition to channel imbalance, we must also consider
the allied phonomenon of channel blockage. Channel
blockage is a condition that occurs when the routes to the
top in any division or function are blocked by immobile
managers. In this same corporation, upper middle managers in accounting functions and allied responsibilities were
blocking the upward mobility of managers below them.
This was discovered by the number of managers in lower
positions who either quit the company and either attempted to leverage or applied to central personnel for a

transfer. Because of both channel imbalance and blockage, managers can have their upward mobility rates severely curtailed. One of the conditions of mobility is being in the right channel.

It must be noted that channel blockage may be partly a channel imbalance, but not all imbalance is a function of blockage. There are blockers even in highly mobile channels.

The generation of future managers now in college will eventually collide with this large and relatively immobile group of managers occupying the middle levels of the corporation. During the last decade, the new technology required the new skills of the college graduate. He has been moved relatively fast and has left behind many managers in the lower and middle management ranks. As he has come through these blocks and imbalances, he has had to learn how to work for a shelf sitter and how to supervise him. But the passed-over generation has watched in pain its own eclipse and has for some time become increasingly restive. The college graduate today will find shelf sitters in imbalanced and blocked channels more difficult to handle both as superiors and subordinates.

The problem for the next decade is how to best use this middle management spread of shelf sitters. Many corporations have been reluctant to fire a manager whose upward mobility has become arrested and level of performance has lowered appreciably. A kind of humanitarian ethic has developed during the last two decades that, if a manager has given the best years of his life to the corporation, he will not be fired or have his financial security jeopardized. In some corporations, a manager who has spent twenty years with the firm has had to work at getting fired. He has become what is commonly referred to as "burn proof." An affluent economy can afford to take out this kind of fire insurance on senior managers. The recent slowdown in the economy has caused many corporations to ask if such a policy is wise and if it is good for the individual and the corporation that he has this high degree of financial security.

If a major economic recession does occur, the corporation may be forced to delete from the rolls vast numbers of shelf sitters and to acquire from all who remain greater degrees of skill and proficiency. What will be called for in order to achieve these objectives is a higher level of managerial skill than corporations have required during the past two decades.

What this means is that the mobile manager is going to have to learn how to work more effectively with managers who are shelf sitters. The tremendous number of middle managers represented by the wide girth of the light bulb may prove to be a formidable barrier to the next generation that seeks to break through them on their way to the top. Let us look more closely at the shelf sitter in relation to arrested mobility.

Arrested Mobility

What the mobile manager fears most is the arresting of upward mobility. What he fears least is the greater responsibility of higher positions. If he has had a sustained pattern of mobility, he has been conditioned to expect the unexpected, to absorb the new and apply the old. He can tangibly lock-on to a new job, regardless of the dexterity required. He can work off his fears and anxieties by hard work and intense concentration. Except insofar as high performance contributes to mobility, he can exert little control over his mobility rate. He fears that which he can least control. Arrested mobility may occur in numerous forms, four types of which are illustrated below:

Four Types of Arrested Mobility

		PA	AE
Manager	A	A+*	P+†
Manager	B	A+	P—
Manager	C	A—	P+
Manager	D	A—	P—

*Aspiration.   †Potential.

The column headings PA and AE refer respectively to private aspirations and authorities' evaluation. Private aspirations are those of the manager—what he would actually like to do. Authorities' evaluation is a composite of his superiors' impressions as to whether he has promotable talent.

For an example, let us refer to Manager A. Under column PA, the A+ indicates that he has great hope of continuing his present rate of mobility or of increasing it. In short, he wants to go higher.

Under column AE, the P+ rating for the same manager indicates that his superiors believe that he has talent, expect him to achieve higher levels of performance, and are willing to advance him as fast as the opportunity allows.

Similarly, the rating of A— under PA indicates that the manager, in this case C or D, is satisfied to remain at the same place or level and wishes to conserve his gains.

A P— under column AE means that the authorities have judged this manager to be at the peak of his ability and do not expect any sudden change in his pattern of performance.

Let us now reconsider manager A. The reader may ask why he is classified as an arrested mobility type. The reason is that movement to the top is never an unbroken series of promotions, but rather an uneven series of fast moves spliced unpredictably with slow ones. At any given time he may appear to be arrested. The corporation cannot always program people in keeping with their developmental and mobility needs at any given time. There are always some managers who are performing below their mobility and developmental levels. For example, at least one out of every three executives in the arrival stage is performing responsibilities that have become routine to him. He is positioned to be ready for the call, but he must wait for someone to retire, to transfer, or to be promoted. Affluent corporations have a kind of managerial bank with many waiting to be cashed and drawn into action and others destined to be deposited. Rich is the corporation that has large talent deposits, although these will nevertheless depreciate if they are left uninvested.

Men in this talent bank are not truly arrested mobility types. They are mobile because they are identified as resources for future contingencies and emergencies. The arrested mobility type is one who is identified as having reached his peak, and who will no longer be expected to pull heavier responsibilities. This manager is reclining on a shelf, solving routine problems that require little or no effort. Between the executive who is "in" the bank and who is out of the line of action, there are two kinds of managers.

The first is the marginal type. He has made a few mistakes that superiors have evaluated as major. He cannot be relied upon for consistently high performance and has lost whatever trust he has accumulated. His condition is one of marginality because superiors are not certain what to do with him. They may decide to give him another chance. They may overpromote him or give him assignments that exceed his developmental level. He may fail, and if he does under this condition of high exposure, he may become a vulnerable type.

This second type of manager, the vulnerable executive, is in such a precarious position that if he makes one more mistake he is placed on the shelf, away from any action that is crucial or vital. The tragedy for him is that there are always scorekeepers. They overevaluate this final mistake to the extent that he loses all sponsorship. He is transferred to a job that has no exposure, and little visibility. At this point he becomes a fullfledged shelf sitter in their eyes but not in his own. Let us look at our table of arrested mobility types once again. Notice that manager B wants to go higher (A+). He has not yet given up. Managers who have been conditioned by visibility never give up entirely their hope of going higher. Some will refuse to read the intended and unintended messages that indicate their loss of mobility, namely, the decreasing amount of exposure, visibility, challenging assignments, and opportunities to evaluate and nominate. Finally there is the tendency for superiors to overevaluate their mistakes and underevaluate their successes.

Manager B's difficulty is that he may not know who the superiors are who hold negative evaluations of him. Only a few, if any, actually inform him of their true opinion of him. Nor does he always know why he is valued negatively. What causes him to hold out hope is the ambiguity of the messages that flow from the evaluators. The more desperate he is for visibility, the more he reads into these messages. He can easily be misinformed by the literal, benign message. It is odd, but the more the corporation gives respect to a person, the more difficult it is to assess the information of his evaluators. A smile that comes from a superior's desire to make him feel comfortable may be interpreted as a cue that he is not arrested after all. The same smile may be interpreted the next time as an attempt to patronize him.

Another reason that he keeps alive the hope for mobility is the tendency for superiors to be very mobile and to come and go frequently. The shelf sitter knows that in a mobile organization a manager can be on a shelf one day and in the stream of action the next. He may want to impress the next superior, and the next, and so on.

A third reason for the shelf sitter not to accept his fate is that managers who are effective only at the present level may be transferred to a different position on the same level. A corporation may move a shelf sitter laterally and geographically. With each move, he has a chance to gain exposure and visibility. There is always a chance that he may pick up support or even sponsorship.

Some shelf sitters acquire an attitude of sour grapes. They rationalize that they are better off where they are, that life above them is excruciatingly stressful, and that the advantages do not offset the risks. In actual fact, the men who move to the top have been given gradual increases in stress, and with each round of stress they achieve mastery that enables them to undertake a greater amount. Of course, some mobile managers move up too fast and fail to absorb the stress or handle it predictably, but most do not make the big leaps that exceed their stress tolerances.

We shall assume that manager C has not rationalized his immobility. He literally feels useful and honorable at his level and does not want to improve his lot, but his private aspirations, or the lack thereof, are not legitimate in many organizations. Mobile superiors do not really understand the manager who is happy where he is. The corporation puts considerable capital resources into the development of managers at any level and does not usually feel that the manager has the privilege of turning down a promotion. To do so is to say that the company has no right to gain a profit from its investment. Besides, the manager who is contented is more difficult to get to jump. Mobile managers maintain that men hungry for promotion are more controllable. For several reasons, then, superiors want the sole prerogative of positive or negative promotion decisions.

The only manager who is immune from the anxiety of mobility is manager D. He does not want to go higher and he cannot. He is viewed as performing effectively at his present level, and he enjoys the thought of staying at his present level or in his present position. The problem of this shelf sitter is that he can easily become a marginal effective who does just enough to hold his present position and conserve his present gains. Our corporations are riddled with marginal effectives, presenting their superiors with difficult problems. Shelf sitters who resign themselves to their fates tend gradually to decrease their investment of energy, but they hope to increase their benefits and rewards. The superior must help them to do a good job so that they do not become marginal effectives, but he does not want to rekindle in them false hopes of going higher.

The tolerances are very close. The motivation to do a good job is related to the motivation to go higher. It is difficult to increase the one without increasing the other. Many superiors, therefore, take little action in regard to manager D and instead concentrate their efforts on the more developmental managers A and C.

Of course, the evaluations of superiors are subject to errors. There are many shelf sitters who are developmental but who have been mistakenly shoved aside. The longer they stay in positions with little visiposure, the more difficult it is to show developmental talent. Many shelf sitters have more competency and talent than their reputations suggest. The corporation that is hard pressed for managerial talent will do well to search for it within the corporation. There should be a policy to keep track of shelf sitters, and after a number of years at a given level, some should be promoted on the principle of testing the validity of the evaluations made. The results may be pleasantly surprising. It is less costly to promote some shelf sitters now and then than to bring along young men to levels above them. Even if the success rate is one or two out of ten, the fallout advantage will justify the effort.

Of course, not all men can go to the top. Organizations need capable men at all levels. Some men may not be corporate material, but they can do more than they are now doing.

Manager D can easily move from the status of a managerial effective to a non-effective. He is often called a loser or an "it" or a non-person. In a way, corporation life is the flux from being an "in" to becoming an "it." Many managers fail to value the feeling of a person who once held the reins of authority and power and who now has no presence or weight at all. These non-persons are seen but not heard, patronized but not evaluated. The "it" can make mistakes with immunity. He holds little danger for the superior or the corporation because he is performing the most perfunc-

tory of responsibilities. The shelf sitter's mistakes are underevaluated, as are the mistakes of crucial subordinates,
but for different reasons.

One of the ways that a mobile manager may have his
upward route arrested is by becoming a subordinate to a
shelf sitter. He often refers to this kind of superior as a
blocker. If the blocker knows that he is not going any-
where, he may attempt to hold down the mobile subordinate. He is more apt to do this if there is a wide discrepan-
cy in age between him and his subordinate. Superiors by
the very fact of their presence tend to block both the exposure and visibility of their subordinates. Some do this
more than others. The mobile superior will tend to inform
his superior of the excellent work and results of his crucial
subordinates. Theirs is a reciprocal relationship of work,
praise, and support from which both superior and subordinates benefit. The shelf sitter, in contrast, aggressively
tends to minimize the visiposure of all subordinates, especially those that threaten his security. High performance
may shake his feelings of security as well as the high mobility of a subordinate.

The reason that a mobile manager may be assigned to
work for a shelf sitter is because the responsibilities of such
a position may call for exceptional talent at times, or his
weaknesses may require the offsetting talents of a mobile
manager. Shelf sitters have little power of nomination;
they must accept what is assigned to them. More than any
other manager, they tend to look for themselves in their
subordinates who are usually supplementary types although occasionally, some may become crucial to the limited effectiveness of their superiors. It is seldom that they
are without their favorites. Their deficiencies and weaknesses and those of their favorite subordinates may have
few, if any, offsetting or balancing skills.

Mobile managers with complementary skills may be assigned to balance team effort but their very strengths
threaten the shelf sitters and their favorite subordinates.

They may consciously or unconsciously attempt to subvert their manager's effectiveness. Shelf sitters may move concertedly against them, depriving them of the necessary information and support to do their assignments. Shelf sitters may assign their mobile subordinates work that does not utilize their strengths. As a result of these antagonisms, a shelf sitter and a mobile subordinate may clash either openly or covertly. When this happens, the shelf sitter will attempt to seize upon the difficulty as evidence that the manager is not qualified or willing to assume the role of a subordinate. The sponsor of the subordinate may move him rather than move the shelf sitter. If he does, the shelf sitter has been successful and remains a block to any future mobile manager.

Sometimes a mobile manager may be assigned to a blocker to experience directly the ineffective style of a poor manager. Some of the most valuable experiences of a mobile manager come from having to expose his talents to a shelf sitter and from seeing the various forms of reaction. Sometimes a mobile manager may be assigned to help unblock a route that is occupied by a shelf sitter. In such a case, the mobile manager must attempt to overcome the handicaps mentioned above and win the shelf sitter over to him. This is a fine exercise in which the mobile manager has everything to gain and nothing to lose. If he is successful, he will replace the superior, open up a route and gain invaluable experience besides. If he fails, he will learn what he did wrong, but because of sponsorship his mistakes will be underevaluated. He will simply be moved to another job. Seldom will he replace the shelf sitter if it comes to open battle because the corporation sets a high priority on obedience to superior authority and will not allow even a shelf sitter to be overthrown. Few palace revolts are successful for this reason. In rare cases will the battle between the mobile manager and the shelf sitter result in the summary removal of the latter. When this does happen, the battle has not usually been overt and public, and the corporation can remove the loser without setting a bad precedent. One thing is certain, a battle between a shelf sitter and a subordinate who has little or no sponsorship is never decided in favor of the latter. In fact, two shelf sitters in over-under relationships can battle for extended periods of time before either one is hurt radically. The manager who stands to gain the most from a clash with a shelf sitter is the one who has sponsorship, and he can best impress his sponsor by acting prudently. Essentially this means that he should not embarrass his sponsor by a public demonstration of his differences with his shelf sitting superior.

Another reason a clash seldom results in summary removal of the superior is that paradoxically shelf sitters are needed at all levels. Without shelf sitters, there could be few mobile managers. Not all can be either one or the other. Moving shelf sitters every time they have difficulty with subordinates will destroy whatever dignity and effectiveness that they may have. In addition, the mobile manager is given an acute means of dealing with his superior to the sacrifice of acquiring the more mobile and organizationally useful skills.

All of which tends to suggest that at any given time, many mobile managers are not crucial subordinates to their superiors. They are temporarily engaged in a difficult struggle to enhance the overall effectiveness of a superior and his team of subordinates. This is a developmental exercise which holds many potential advantages to the corporation, to the shelf sitter, and to the subordinate.

To become effective and mobile, the manager must have before him models of effective managerial behavior. He stands to gain immensely from trying out their ideas and techniques and judiciously rating them on the basis of results. There are superiors that represent models of corporate behavior, whose styles reflect the values and priorities of successful men. A representative model may be at any level in the corporation. He may exist at the lower middle management level because he has modelled himself after a superior. The manager who has high visiposure of both lateral and vertical types is more capable of spotting a genuine model from a superficial one. He can see that his model's behavior is achieving the kind of results that gain the highest rewards, one of which is mobility itself. The most mobile managers tend to gravitate toward representative behavior.

The modes of representative behavior are manifold. Contrary to many reports, there are a number of ways of behaving that are at the same time individual and yet still representative. Innovative behavior is what helps to give the manager positive exposure. Occasionally, his superior may be mobile and not representative or not a model. This superior is successfully innovating; he is acting differently yet keeping the support of his superiors. But the subordinate may not know that he can safely attempt to model himself after his superior or he may be reluctant because he has sufficiently high visiposure to see that his superior's behavior is unusual. Because it takes time to see a positive connection between his superior's behavior and high support, the subordinate may play it safe.

If the manager does not have high visiposure, he may fail to see how unique and controversial is the behavior of his superior. He may develop into unrepresentative behavior and go the way of his superior. If the superior succeeds, the manager may also; if he fails, so may the manager.

In the early stages of his managerial career, a subordinate needs to model himself after somebody. He may adopt the mode of a superior who unknown to him is actually a shelf sitter. First level managers make this mistake quite often. They may become so useful to their superior that they become crucial to his effectiveness. It may be a while before the subordinates realize that they have become too much like shelf sitters. Because a subordinate has learned essentially weak skills and unrepresentative behavior, his potential for development may be discounted by lateral and vertical superiors. This illustrates that blind conformity and imitation are dangerous.

Most corporations know that a young manager tends to become very impressed by his superior's qualities. To keep him from learning any one mode of managerial behavior, the alert company will give a first level manager a chance to work with several superiors before he is discounted. Based upon this reasoning, laterals may occur commonly at lower levels. It is reasonable to expect that a first level manager who fails dramatically will receive a demotion rather than a lateral transfer, regardless of the effectiveness of the superior. The presumption is that all superiors are effective enough for the subordinate who has sufficient managerial potential to avoid dramatic failure. On the other hand, that all superiors are effective enough to ensure the development of potential talent is never presumed. In other words, if a new manager fails, it is because he is unsuited for managerial responsibility. If he is evaluated as marginal, it may be because he needs more development. This may include a different position or a new superior or both. If a first level manager dramatically exceeds his superior's fondest expectations, it is because he has great talent and, hence, great potential. At this point, the manager may be exposed to positions and to superiors who know how to draw out his potential talent and develop it further. He may be given a lateral transfer or a promotion. The principle seems to be that dramatic success or failure is due to the individual, but marginal success or failure may be due to a poor superior. Subordinates to several superiors will help to sharpen the relative contribution of the subordinate and his superior to his performance.

During the early stages of his career, the future president does not reveal in his managerial behavior exceptional talent or dramatic results. He learns efficiently, however, from his mistakes which are not of the kind usually ascribed to the lack of talent and potential, but are simply entrance mistakes. There are errors that new managers can learn to avoid by exposure to behavior of effective superiors.

It is a fact that some of the best superiors for instructing new managers are shelf sitters of the kind represented by Manager D. They recognize that their advancement in the corporation has terminated, and they have become adjusted to their positions and levels. Often, they have the patience to impart their wisdom, the age to enjoy the coming and going of young men, and the security to do fairly well what they please. This includes singling out an occasional manager who has high potential and putting an extraordinary amount of effort into his training and preparation. This kind of shelf sitter is invaluable in the help that he can give to a young man who may as a result gain a permanent foothold on the corporate ladder. A shelf sitter may be a developer even though he is not developmental himself. A corporation that knows its range of shelf sitters may route developmental types through their departments. The mobile manager has left behind many shelf sitters who have helped him to become effective. There are few presidents who cannot point to several shelf sitters and say, "He became a turning point in my career." To these men we may ascribe the term, crucial superiors. This includes both mobile and immobile types. The mobile manager leaves no stone unturned in his desire to gain experience and skill. He is often heard to say, "I have never worked for a superior from whom I have not learned much." In sum, shelf sitters who either block or enhance development are crucial figures in the world of the mobile manager.

Mobility Fatigue

The high rate of mobility has created a set of symptoms which may be called mobility fatigue. The key symptom is a lack of energy to fulfill even the normal responsibilities of managing. Energy has two basic forms, physical and psychological. The former is easily recognizable and is evident when a person can freely exert effort and has a high level of endurance and stamina. Psychological energy is less apparent and is most recognizable in the form of enthusiasm, drive, ambition, and responsiveness. We may say that the manager with psychological energy is motivated by his work.

Physical and psychological energy are really two sides of the same coin. When physical energy falls, so does the level of psychological energy. This principle is illustrated by the fact that one seems to have more physical energy when one does what he enjoys. The moment he anticipates doing what he is motivated to do, he gets a burst of physical energy. The satisfaction that comes from doing what one enjoys replenishes the physical energy that was used. A man can work hard all day, and if he enjoys what he does, he will have the same amount of energy the next morning after rest, food, and relaxation. But no amount of the latter will adequately replenish the physical energy used during the day in work that is uninteresting. Psychological energy calls for the release of physical energy, which is replenished by satisfaction. The latter maintains the level of psychological energy. A man can work hard every day and live to a ripe old age, as did in our time such men as Churchill and Adenauer and still keep high levels of strength and motivation. Man was meant to do what he enjoys and to find enjoyment in what he has to do.

Energy fatigue occurs when this principle is violated. A man does not need to live a well-rounded life to sustain a level of high energy. But he must find compensation when he cannot replenish energy in work that is unsatisfying. A well-rounded life is a necessity for the man who must work at a job that is not challenging; it is a luxury for the man who has great challenge in his work.

Managers are usually high energy types. They have a surplus of physical and psychological energy. Each round of success replenishes and keeps them strong and motivated to achieve higher goals. But there is for everybody a threshold of diminishing return, at which point the energy rate is decreasing. A person may be working harder than he is deriving satisfaction. If he is not allowed to find compensation, he may become exhausted physically and psychologically.

We have said that energy fatigue is the chief symptom of mobility fatigue. This is not to say that mobility fatigue is the only problem in which energy fatigue is the key symptom. Energy fatigue may be caused by many different problems, one of which is the stress and strain of mobility.

It is evident that mobility fatigue is a negative reaction to mobility. It is likely to set in when the manager is moved too fast to absorb the changes in his work, family, and community roles. He simply cannot keep up in all these areas. What he does never gets done completely, or is not rewarding or is too often another person's idea. He may do it out of a sense of duty or devotion, but he seems to be on a hopeless treadmill.

Some managers display a low threshold for ambiguity. When they get involved in too many activities that cannot be finished, they lose their sense of challenge. Others can live in situations that are always emerging, that never stand still, and enjoy it all tremendously. Their span of attention is wide, and their feeling of effectiveness is highest when they have twelve projects going at the same time. They can mentally shift gears, pursue diverse objectives, plan for the unexpected, and recover when the worst that can happen does happen. Yet, somehow, they always land on their feet without any loss of equilibrium. When the word comes to abandon one project and start a new assignment, they have no feeling of being mistreated or cheated.

Mobility and ambiguity are near synonyms. If the threshold for tolerating ambiguity is low to begin with or is driven down by unfortunate experiences, the call to a new assignment will arouse feelings of anxiety and dread. Energy released in new positions that are dreaded will not be replenished. In a state of decreasing energy, the manager may make mistakes that could prove disastrous. These mistakes may be caused by subtle decreases in the functioning of the senses. For example, if X is the amount of energy required to hear, it is estimated that 10X is the amount of energy required to listen. A drop in energy level may cause the manager to miss subtle cues that might greatly change his behavior.

When managers make mistakes caused by energy fatigue, they blame mobility and perhaps rightly so. If they are demoted or arrested, they may appeal to the defense mechanism of rationalization. They are often heard to say, "Oh, well, I'm glad that I'm not going higher. The additional salary and responsibility are not worth the cost to me." This point is usually true. In that state of mind they will be expending energy unproductively and inefficiently. This rationalization when adhered to may actually save them from a greater degree of energy fatigue.

The corporation, however, may not fully understand the symptoms of mobility fatigue. If the superior misjudges the manager's level of energy, he may unknowingly contribute to his mobility fatigue by a lateral demotion or even promotion. In each of these reassignments there is a kind of mobility, and to a manager already suffering from mobility fatigue, any one change may be too much for him to absorb. A demotion is difficult enough for any manager to absorb, but if he is suffering from mobility fatigue, his overreaction to it may border on irrationality. Oddly enough, the overreaction may also occur at the point of a lateral or promotion. The author has seen managers hand in their resignations at the point of a promotion. The shocked reaction by the superior attested to the lack of understanding of the subordinate's condition. Mobility fatigue seeks the cessation of all mobility: lateral, upward, downward, including radical changes in assignments in the same position. The manager obviously needs a rest. He needs to be left alone or he will commit mistakes that meet the level of incompetency, and which may ruin his future career.

The author has seen the symptoms of mobility fatigue disappear through inactivity and isolation, but only when the superior is insightful enough to inform the subordinate that he is being sidelined temporarily because he is a valuable member of the team. A good dose of inactivity and isolation may allow him to tidy up his home and community life, get back his self-confidence, and give him the desire to get going again. When his drive has returned, so will the physical energy to attend carefully to his work.

The problem is that many superiors are not trained to diagnose mobility fatigue. The mistakes that the manager may make are interpreted as incompetency. Too often the superior assumes that the manager has peaked out at the top of his ability. The word goes out that the manager is non-developmental and should be left alone. If the manager is left alone, he may recover and want to regain mobility, which may not be forthcoming, however, because of the mistakes in diagnosis by his superiors.

This presents a different problem. The manager is once again full of energy and has nowhere to release it. He finds his present job uninteresting and wants to move on to more challenging assignments. Every unit of energy expended fails to replenish itself and the manager falls into a condition called secondary mobility fatigue. The manager grows tired of waiting for mobility.

Secondary mobility fatigue can produce disastrous results. For example, a manager regained his drive, but grew impatient with his lack of mobility. He went to the superior who believed that he had peaked and asked for an explanation for his being put on a shelf. The superior, wanting to justify his judgment, denied the accusation in the usual manner which is to face the subordinate and to say with a most serious face, "No job here is unimportant. If it were, we would have eliminated it or delegated it to someone below you." The manager received this treatment and was forced to give up his attempt to regain his mobility. What he did not know was that the superior interpreted this behavior to be further evidence that he was not capable of holding a higher position. A stalemate had been reached; the manager was desperate. He could not explain his situation to *his* superior, who, in turn could not explain his judgment to *his* subordinate. As a result, this manager left the firm shortly thereafter, and ironically enough received two quick promotions in the new firm, much to the dismay of his former superior.

There are many managers who suffer intensely from secondary mobility fatigue while they are waiting for a promotion. Meanwhile, they do not display in their present jobs qualities which can be recognized as promotable. At least one out of three arrested mobility types reclines on neatly prepared shelves with great expectations. After some time these managers silently vow not to expend any more energy than necessary to conserve their gains. They await the corporation to rescue them from their entrapment, but they will not take a hand in their own extrication. Perhaps from the standpoint of energy this tactic is wise since by keeping their energy in line with their opportunities, they avoid severe energy fatigue.

Suppose, however, that the manager decides to chance the investment of huge amounts of energy in the hope that a promotion may come. One of three possible results is likely to occur. The first is that he may change the superior's judgment and receive his eagerly sought promotion. In this case, everything is fine and the crisis has passed, at least for now temporarily. The second possibility is that by rearranging his pattern of investment, he may actually come to enjoy his present position. If he does, his gamble will have paid off in the form of energy replenishment. He may become his old self again and may even get the additional bonus of a promotion. It is also possible that a promotion could be negatively received at this point. The third condition is that he will fail to receive a promotion or to increase substantially the satisfaction derived from his work. He may develop a chronic case of mobility fatigue.

The key symptom of chronic mobility fatigue is a bitter, almost vindictive attitude toward anybody or anything that smacks of change of any kind, including mobility. He becomes a confirmed reactionary and develops a philosophy that supports this kind of behavior in public. The true rebel in a society where the only certainty is change itself is the individual who resists change, including mobility. The conformist adopts the dominant motif of his generation. Today, the manager who centers his life style upon mobility is the conformist. We shall refer to this conformist as mobicentric.

Chapter VI

THE MOBICENTRIC MANAGER

The high rate of upward mobility will continue to sweep men to the top in unprecedented numbers. It has already brought the youngest generation of executives to the top and behind them is a new style of manager, whose implications are too new to be properly assessed, but whose values are becoming clearly evident. Although a census has not been taken of this new manager, the mobicentric, mobilography has revealed the essential characteristics of the men who belong to this category. The mobicentric manager conforms to the theme of mobility which we have noted is ascendant in the world of the big business executive. He displays a style of managing that is based upon being both mobility directed and mobility bright. Let us examine first the condition of mobility directedness.

Mobility Directedness

It was common to describe the pre-mobile generation of businessmen as directed by the need to achieve. They were said to worship the goddess of success, but was this indeed the case? Many studies affirmed that the big businessman typically sought interesting and challenging tasks, and to perform them with skill and dispatch. He believed that competency would be rewarded by upward mobility.

Because of his high need to achieve, he attempted to make things happen. In this event-making quality was contained the ancillary drive to seek positions at higher levels. The steps up the corporate ladder represented increasing degrees of challenge. Presumably, if work became more interesting with each step down the ladder, the manager would work to descend rather than ascend. The direction of mobility was not important as long as it brought jobs that satisfied the manager's achievement needs. In this sense, the manager went where the action was as though he had a built in homing device that always kept him on a challenging target. In this sense, he was directed towards achievement.

The results thus far obtained from mobilography have brought perspective to our analysis of the pre-mobile generation. To them mobility was a means of maintaining a high degree of achievement satisfaction. The manager was easily bored by repetition and routine and sought mobility largely, if not entirely, because mobility brought new and more challenging tasks. There was relatively little fun in movement itself; the fun was found in performance. The essential tie between the manager and the corporation was work performance, and he sought in his work the necessary prerequisite for higher and challenging responsibilities. Of course, mobility was appreciably slower then than it is now, and the manager never conceived of the possibility that mobility could become an end rather than a mere means.

A high rate of lateral and vertical mobility has inverted the ends of achievement and the means. It is apparent that the new generation is still motivated to achieve, but achievement is not performing a task and hoping for the opportunity of performing at a high level of challenge. To the mobicentric, the highest form of achievement is to become and stay mobile. Performance is a means, not an end, and is represented by activity that was alien to the pre-mobile generation. Performance today means to arrive, to perform, and to depart; it means compressing experience, movement around as well as up, management by objectives, project and task force management; it means lateral mobility, outspan positions, role reversal, tandem and dual assignments; and it means geographical and social mobility. In mobility the manager finds a challenge incomparably greater than that faced by the previous generation. The new generation finds that mobility brings competency, whereas the pre-mobile generation believed that competency brought mobility.

It should be emphasized that mobility directedness does not represent a superficial change of behavior. The personality of the mobicentric is centered around mobility. This means that he is a different person. He not only manages differently; he lives differently. He gears his family and community relations to the pattern of arriving, performing, and departing. Among his friends are people who are usually members of his corporation because they can provide him with instant social friendship. And the friends he makes of non-corporation people invariably are mobile types who know how to make the most of their social relationships during a short period of time. With everyone he likes to be pleasant but a little distant, and to avoid people who are unaccustomed to his style of living.

To his children and his wife he teaches the pleasures of mobility. He believes that children can be better movers than parents, and that they can learn to be mobile or immobile. The author overheard the son of a mobile manager ask his father when they were going to move again, because the son had noticed that they had been in the same community almost two years. Contrary to the rumors that business executives do not know their children, mobicentrics tend to place high value on family life. Their frequent moves cause them to rely more upon each other because the family is the only secure refuge. During an era when the family is breaking down, the mobicentric manager typically enjoys a close relationship to his family. His family life suggests that a family that moves together stays together.

Of course, there are mobicentrics that do not enjoy family and community life, but there were also members of the pre-mobile generation who did not have fun with their children or enjoy their communities. The author took at random one hundred very mobile managers and the same number of immobiles and discovered that the latter had a higher incidence of divorce and separation. Although this number is too small to develop reliable statistics, the possibility may be that mobility is not the cause of the breaking down of family and marriage, but, rather the cause of stress and strain. Mobility can produce stress in some men in sufficient degrees to be a factor contributing to divorce and family deterioration. However, the mobility directed manager is not apt to become mobility fatigued. He is apt to enjoy mobility and to treat it as achievement opportunity. To his family he teaches the same values.

The mobicentric acquires a cosmopolitan orientation in contrast to the older generation's provincialism. In the home of a mobile manager, the author saw a little plaque with the inscription, "Join the XYZ corporation and see the world." A cosmopolitan orientation brings to the mobile manager a broad view of community and national problems. The author has observed many times that the overviews of mobicentrics contribute fresh and objective information to the various community organizations to which they belong.

In short, the manager before this era of rapid mobility looked to settling down in an office and gradually mastering the many routines and challenges. The office gave him his sense of identity. The picture that he associated in his mind with work was that of an executive about fifty years of age with his coat off, leaning over a desk with pencil in hand, making some kind of draft or memo. The picture with which the mobicentric identifies is a young man dressed in a business suit walking to a plane with a brief case in his hand. He acquires his sense of identity from the fast rate by which he moves in his corporation and society. He believes that the future holds great challenge and he lives for what it will bring. He believes that tomorrow will be better than today, and that although he lives only once, if he lives right he needs to live only once.

Mobility Brightness

To properly direct his mobility drive, the manager must have a second quality; he must be mobility bright. By this we mean that he must be knowledgeable about the ways of mobility. There are managers who are mobility directed but not mobility bright. They seek to acquire and enhance their mobility, but lack the necessary wisdom. Of course, a necessary condition of mobility brightness is to be mobility directed. But unless the manager has had rapid mobility in general and compression experience in particular, the manager cannot be truly knowledgeable about the mobile world. Then, too, some managers learn better than others. They experience more efficiently and draw useful principles and generalizations from their experiences. They have learned how to learn. Of all the things that they could see, they tend to see precisely those things that give maximum expression to their mobility drive. They screen out the kind of information that men less wise in the ways of mobility tend to accept. In short, the mobility drive serves as a gyroscope that keeps the managers on a steady course, but first the course must be set by his mobility brightness.

The mobility bright manager knows that movement up the corporate ladder brings gradual changes in the expectations of the people with whom he must work. These changes may amount to shifts in priorities of what is valued or believed or these changes may represent entirely new beliefs and attitudes. The differences among expectations and beliefs between two adjoining levels of managers are not as noticeable as between two levels of managers separated by one or two levels. As the manager moves through the layers of the corporation, he attempts to notice the subtle, incremental changes in his environment. In the language of the mobile manager, he reads his environment. He draws a mental picture, a map, of the exact nature of his terrain. His facility to read and to map must be keenly developed in order for the manager to make the necessary adjustments. He must also read and map in order to determine how best to apply his efforts to gain the greatest payoffs. Let the reader not be misled; the mobility bright manager is not a conformist. He behaves according to the requirements of assuming initiative and becoming recognized for his results. If he conforms, it is for the purpose and to the extent of gaining the opportunities and resources to initiate and innovate.

The point is that the mobility bright manager can see differences emerge from one level to another that miss the eye of the less sensitive manager. A careful analysis of these differences reveals that the upper management (or executive) department is different from lower management (or managerial) department in the following ways:

1. Executives* have more established identities than managers. They know better who they are and feel more confident of where they are going. Another way to say this is that they are more self-involved in their careers and carry their responsibilities more into both their successes and failures. They have less of the employee mentality and more of the professional. Executives see themselves as professional people who sell their services to a particular corporation and who are prepared to leave when given a greater professional opportunity in another corporation. They interact with each other in a spirit of rapport, realizing that the concept of face is important to all. Because authority differences among levels of executives tend to be minimal, they tend to influence each other by means of conversational, informal suggestions.

What may appear to the mobility dull manager to be voices of trivial opposition, are in fact the voices of constrained and subtle rebutting of crucial differences, couched in an impersonal way in order to help save face for their colleagues. Successes and failures are also presented in an impersonal way for the same reason of saving face. In all organizations and at all levels, people find a target when

---

*Executives are men in the arrival stage at the top of the corporation, and managers are below them in the developmental stages of middle management.

things go wrong and lay all the trouble to it although there is less tendency to find scapegoats at higher levels. Executives are more concerned about what went wrong than who caused it to do so.

To put it in different terms, executives' mistakes are evaluated in terms of objective consequences. To say that executives are less petty is to hide the fact that they can become irritated by nuances the same as managers. But they are prohibited by their sense of rapport to expose their peers' mistakes unless these mistakes make objectively provable differences in achieving corporate aims and goals. Also, executives are less quick to judge each other because their decisions span longer periods of time and what may initially appear to be mistakes may with time turn out to be major breakthroughs.

Executives tend to use a feather-light touch with their subordinates and peers. The heavy hand of the lower positioned manager is frowned upon at high corporate levels. The term style is often used to mean the ability to say and do almost anything without antagonizing others. People tend to work better when they do not have to work at saving face.

To be mobility bright also means to present oneself in a manner becoming to the dignity and stature of the superiors above. It means to behave as though the manager were at a higher level than his present one. For men in the arrival (top) level, it is to reveal a style that is becoming to a corporation president. The principle is that the closer one moves to the office of the president, the more executives show in their manners and conduct the style representative of the character of the corporation. They know that they are viewed by managers below them as representative models. They attempt individually and collectively to mirror the best manners and morals of the corporation.

(2) The mobicentric manager knows that mobility brings high risk. Success is not measured by the distance from first level management. He knows that the closer he gets to the

top, the more likely is failure to occur. Few men arrive at the top without putting their careers on the line. The mobicentric is prepared to risk his career, but is careful to pick the right time and place. When career risk is involved, the executive realizes that if the decisions go against him, he may be removed, and if not, he will have to remove himself from the corporation to preserve his sense of dignity.

Both executives and managers incur risk to some extent every day because their decisions are based upon uncertainties. A typical decision is based upon 10 percent of the facts that would become available if the executive had twice as much time to make his decision. But these kinds of risks are not what is referred to as career risks. The executive who makes a major contribution does so in the face of intense opposition. During the many conferences that are set up to discuss his pet project, the ball bounces back and forth between colleagues that support his idea and those that object to it. In most cases, the deciding factor becomes the executive's sheer desire to see the program executed and his willingness to stake his whole career on the outcome. If the results fall short of what is intended, he will lose his future opportunities to be effective. At this point, he will leverage if he is mobility bright.

3. The mobility bright manager knows that the advantages of leveraging increase the higher he goes up the corporate ladder. Of course, the advantages of staying increase, particularly if the executive is in the bonus and stock option group. However, many an executive has sought to keep the advantages of the latter, only to discover that he will never become president. The mobility bright executive is not deceived by the lock-in provisions by which most large corporations induce their managers and executives to stay with their corporations, regardless of their mobility opportunities. He knows that fewer men each year move to the top by staying in the same firm. The reason for this is

two-fold. The executive who has remained in the same firm most of his career has become a known entity. Both his strengths and weaknesses have become well known. At the top, however, the subordinate's weaknesses are more carefully examined than his strengths. They are weighed more heavily because the assignments are more critical and hold closer tolerances of success and failure. When the tolerances are close between a successful program and a failure, weaknesses are subject to critical analysis. Superiors must know precisely what the executive can and cannot do.

The author has often observed that one executive may be promoted over another because he had less weakness than the other executive. As one president remarked to the author, "When the selection committee gets down to the lint-picking stage, I usually observe that they will accept a man whose strengths and weaknesses are fewer. We will trade off a few less strengths for a few less weaknesses."

However, in most instances an executive's strengths travel better than his weaknesses. The old cliché that an expert is a man fifty miles or more away from his home is certainly appropriate here. Not only do his strengths travel better, but so do his credits. In his home company he may be given only partial credit for an accomplishment because others were also acknowledged to be partly responsible for the success of the project. In another company he may be given total credit. Besides, what may appear as a weakness in his home company may be evaluated as a nuance or even a strength in the other company.

A mobility bright executive is aware of these subtleties and knows how to maximize his strengths and minimize his weaknesses. He may appear to the reader to be playing games, but his reply is that strengths and weaknesses are necessarily relative to the corporation and there is no universal arbiter. Who, then, can say that he is trying to appear to be what he is not. To repeat, there are many executives and managers who are mobility directed and not mobility bright. They want to go higher, but do not know how to. It is important to note that too often they are not aware of the advantages of leveraging.

The mobility directed manager is more interested in his career than in his corporation. He is prepared to leave his corporation if it means he can go higher or faster in another. He aims to go up and not to stay in a given corporation. He is prepared to sacrifice certain advantages of staying in his parent corporation to going higher in another. The increase in the number of mobicentric executives is attested to by the increase in the number of executives who leverage. So great is this increase in leveraging, that some corporate officials are wondering if they should not grant pension rights and stock privileges that are transferable from one corporation to another.

4. The mobility bright manager knows that as he moves higher he must manage better the shelf sitter. Shelf sitters exist at all levels. At the higher reaches of the corporation they can be more of a problem. As one top executive reported, "You cannot afford to ignore men in the upper levels who are not going higher because they have a tenure complex. They know that they are too good for jobs below them, not good enough for jobs above them, and indispensable for jobs that match their skills." At lower levels, the manager can work around shelf sitters, but at higher levels the executive must work with and through them. To ignore them is to incur their wrath but while they can hurt the executive they can help him much more.

The executive is measured in part by how well he can utilize shelf sitters. There are fewer jobs at the top with more people below them. At the top, rapport forbids moving them around without regard to face, and the executive is obliged to use them. Another president said, "Anyone can manage his few crucial subordinates, but it takes a master to manage vice-presidents who are secure for life. Besides, the margins of error are narrower at the top and a bad decision can be bailed out if everyone pitches in, in-

cluding shelf sitters to make the best of it. Here is where
the shelf sitter can make or break a program." Many executives have come to realize that the ultimate difference between success and failure often lies in the acts of shelf
sitters.

5. The mobility bright manager knows that mobility
brings greater logistics support. At lower levels the manager has less opportunity to commandeer the personnel,
tools, and resources that are necessary to success of his
project. He is always working at the margin of inadequate
supply of talent, money, and technical facilities, and hence,
he can be excused if errors occur that are attributable to
these deficiencies. But executives are seldom in this kind of
situation. They can co-opt personnel, tap hidden budgets,
reorganize staff and line personnel. In other words, they
can better squeeze out of the corporation the necessary
logistics support. Their performances are relatively free of
excuses and if they make mistakes, they make them because
of faulty management.

At least this is assumed to be the case in more instances
than not at the executive level. Because of this, the executive has been known to steal, borrow, and trade personnel
and technical resources with seemingly reckless abandon.
His greater span of authority allows him to divert from a
department or division logistical material to execute the
mission that is currently his basic project. His superiors
may not be aware of what other programs were de-
emphasized as long as he is successful in his critical assignment. Few executives can plead that they did not have this
talent or that technical support when things go awry.

The mobility bright executive keeps a steady eye on
surplus and scarce talent and resources. These become
more crucial to his success the higher he goes in the corporation. This means that he must attempt to make and keep
personnel below him vertically and highly exposed to him
laterally. His managerial successes are greatly determined
by how well he reads the roster of managerial talent. If he

maps poorly, he manages poorly. At the same time, he must keep exposed and maintain visibility.

6. The bright manager has a strong desire for visibility and exposure. He studies carefully the expectations and behavior of his superiors for the purpose of evaluating them and modelling himself after them. He prizes most highly multi-level visibility of vertical and lateral types. He utilizes his assignments for the purpose of experimenting with the approaches of his superiors to build a managerial style of his own. He is very capable of reading implicit cues and sensing minor variations in styles.

The mobility bright manager has an equally strong desire to be exposed to superiors who are lateral and vertical to him. He has a tendency to avoid exposure when it is unrepresentative of his behavior or the behavior of his superiors. And he tends to maximize his chances of becoming exposed to the most mobile superiors. This orientation toward superiors largely determines how he selects his assignments when he is given choices. He will always go for assignments that give him high visibility and exposure even though he may suffer in salary or immediate mobility. He knows that in the long run mobility is based upon acquiring and maintaining high visibility and exposure.

In particular, the mobility bright manager is aware of the hazard of fast upward moves that are without transfer of the lateral type. He may even turn down a promotion to accept a lateral assignment in order to avoid the possibility of becoming more mobile than mobility wise. This is the only time he will accept the loss of career time. In short, if he wants to be mobility bright, he must be as wise as his mobility rate requires.

The mobility bright manager intuitively knows that movement up and around is a better indication of mobility than any other pattern of mobility. He does not discount a lateral and does not treat a lateral assignment to be any less challenging than a promotion. Consequently, his superiors see him at his best when he is in a lateral assignment. This exposure may cause him to receive quick promotion. Contrary to what might be assumed, performance in lateral assignments can give more quality exposure than outright promotions.

7. The mobility bright manager is not taken in by the formal organization. He is aware of job title, authority, and hierarchical position, but views them as mere contrivances that hide more than they explain. He is prepared to see the less visible and less audible side of his superiors, chiefly their standing with their peers and superiors. He knows the signs of sponsorship and the less potent skills of evaluation and nomination. He can infer from a minimum of cues who are the centers of power and he seeks to have high visibility and exposure with them. He will assiduously cultivate his standing and opportunities with them and seize every opportunity to learn from them. He will utilize his opportunities in the social world to size up the men who are centers of sponsorship in the corporate world. The mobicentric manager tends to define as powerful in any organization only a few people and these are seldom known by their formal authority, responsibility, job title, or salary. He is not enamored with the trappings of authority and salary and does not seek authority and salary. He goes for influence and power.

To summarize, mobility bright managers notice that competition becomes more intense as they move to the top. However, the desire to cooperate increases commensurately. Executives compete to cooperate and cooperate to compete. They are intensely competitive because more people are in the arrival stage with fewer positions ahead of them. In addition, they have higher expectations because they have come farther. While they work harder to enhance their gains, they work harder to conserve the gains that they already have acquired. Executives are more cooperative because it serves to keep the competitive drive in balance and offset some of the bad effects. But equally important is the fact that the assignments of top level executives by their very nature require more coordinative and interdependent forms of behavior. If the top group is not coordinated, the corporation is not coordinated. In this sense, the executive shows the competitive drive by his efforts to cooperate and he cooperates in order to maintain and enhance his gains. Mobility is based upon the right mixture.

The mobility bright manager knows that as he moves up the corporate ladder, he manages and is managed by men who are more mobility bright than men at lower levels. He knows that he enters an arena in which men's wits are the basic weapons. Their minds are honed to a fine edge and subtle degrees of sharpness can spell the difference between success and failure. The mere presence of an individual with a superior mind gives direction to the battle. To match wits with him is a challenge in itself. The ordinary man cannot understand the challenge represented by succeeding and leaving behind men of worthy skill.

To succeed at the top requires more than getting to the top. The manager must have learned efficiently the lessons taught at middle and lower management levels. The middle management levels serve to filter out the manager who cannot endure the stresses and strains of the executive life, but this screening device is not perfect. A few men may move into the executive ranks who are mobility directed but not sufficiently mobility bright, and some of these will cease to be mobility directed. We have noted in the analysis of shelf sitters that for one reason or another, executives and managers may acquire mobility fatigue and become directed by other values. For the most part, the men who moved to the top during these last two decades of exponential economic growth were both mobility directed and mobility bright. Below these executives are managers on the move who appear to be even more mobicentric.